# Union Policy
## AND THE
# Older Worker

MELVIN K. BERS

GREENWOOD PRESS, PUBLISHERS
WESTPORT, CONNECTICUT

**Library of Congress Cataloging in Publication Data**

Bers, Melvin K
    Union policy and the older worker.

    Reprint of the 1957 ed. published by the Institute
of Industrial Relations, University of California,
Berkeley.
    Includes bibliographical references.
    1.  Age and employment--United States.  2.  Old age
pensions--United States.  3.  Trade-unions--United
States.  I.  Title.
[HD6280.B4 1976]    331.3'98'0973        76-14986
ISBN 0-8371-8655-2

Originally published in 1957 by Institute of Industrial Relations,
University of California, Berkeley

Reprinted with the permission of Institute of Industrial Relations,
University of California, Berkeley

Reprinted in 1976 by Greenwood Press,
a division of Williamhouse-Regency Inc.

Library of Congress Catalog Card Number 76-14986

ISBN 0-8371-8655-2

Printed in the United States of America

# FOREWORD

In 1950, the Institute of Industrial Relations received a sizable grant from the Rockefeller Foundation to conduct a five-year interdisciplinary study of the problem of aging in an industrial society. The plans for the project were formulated under the leadership of Chancellor Clark Kerr, who was then Director of the Institute, and his Associate Director, the late Lloyd H. Fisher. The separate studies which eventually emerged as independent subdivisions of the project dealt with the economic status of the aged, the politics of the aged, the relationship of physiological and psychological age to chronological age, the social and psychological aspects of aging and retirement, employer and union policies toward the older worker, and retirement policy under Social Security legislation. The responsibility for guiding the project in its final stages has fallen chiefly to Dr. Margaret S. Gordon, now Associate Director of the Institute.

Among the groups in a position to influence employment conditions for older workers, unions have assumed an increasingly important role in recent decades. With the spread of collective bargaining to wider sectors of the economy, the terms under which older workers are hired, promoted or reassigned, laid off, and retired have in considerable measure become subject to bilateral negotiation between employers and unions. Meanwhile, government policies have also entered into the picture, particularly in connection with the provisions governing the age at which benefits may be received under the Old Age and Survivors Insurance program. Thus, it is impossible to arrive at a complete picture of the "rules of the labor market" as they affect the employment of the older worker without taking into account the policies of the three major participants in the formulation of these rules—employers, unions, and government agencies.

The present study is concerned with the role of unions in this complex picture. What has been the effect of union policies on employment opportunities for the older worker? Have these policies been consistently directed, as many union spokesmen would argue, toward protecting the older worker's job security? How does the status of the older union member compare with that of the older nonmember? How far have unions been willing to go in insisting on the enforcement of policies which may be resisted by employers? Have union efforts to protect the position of older workers given rise to internal conflict between older and younger union members? And in what ways are such internal developments related to the formation of pension and retirement policies?

These are some of the questions to which the present study is addressed. Unlike some of the other subdivisions of the Rockefeller-financed study of aging, which were organized on a substantial scale, the study of union policies was limited in scope and was essentially a one-man undertaking. Within these limitations, the author has attacked his problem with imagination and the insight of a competently trained labor economist. His findings, as he himself points out, are somewhat tentative. But there is no doubt that they are highly suggestive and will help to stimulate further investigations of the same problem.

Dr. Melvin K. Bers is a former member of the staff of the Institute of Industrial Relations and is now Assistant Professor of Economics at the Carnegie Institute of Technology.

ARTHUR M. ROSS
*Director*

# CONTENTS

# INTRODUCTION[1]

Among the major areas of current interest in the growing literature on aging and the prospect of rapidly increasing numbers of older persons[2] there are two to which the present study of union policy is chiefly relevant. The first resolves itself mainly into questions concerning the volume of "employment opportunity" being made available to older workers. The second has to do with the terms on which the community as a whole offers "retirement" to its older members.

Interest in the problem of employment opportunity available to older workers reflects the concern which has been frequently expressed over the burdens of want, idleness and isolation borne by older persons who are able and willing to go to work but who cannot find it or who are, for various reasons, barred from it. But the personal plight of inactive older workers is only one aspect of the matter. Problems for the community as a whole may arise from their frustration and isolation. At least one writer has called attention to what is viewed as a burden on the nation's political institutions, in the detachment of older persons from the rest of society and their consequent support of organizations designed solely for the advancement of the special interests of the aged.[3]

[1] The author is indebted to Albert J. Abrams, Jeffery Cohelan, Lincoln Fairley, Varden Fuller, Joseph Garbarino, Arthur M. Ross and especially to Mrs. Margaret Gordon for their helpful criticisms of an earlier draft of this paper. Thanks are due also to Curtis Aller and Clark Kerr for valuable suggestions offered in the course of the field work.
[2] In this paper, "older persons" refers to those in the age groups approaching and passing the conventional retirement age of 65.
[3] "... when such group identification tends to become exclusive and all-embracing, when loyalties are increasingly confined to a single identification, when one

Other writers have alluded to the "loss of output" attributable to the inactivity of "prematurely retired" older persons,[4] although a recent study has cast some doubt on the possibility of a substantial increment to output obtainable from this source.[5]

Concern over the "loss of output" associated with the idleness of older persons relates directly to the central issue in the second major sphere of interest, that of the terms on which "retirement" is offered to the community's elderly. The leisure of aged persons is conventionally accepted as standing on a different footing from that of the leisure of younger persons, and this attitude is expressed in a willingness to transfer income in the form of old age or pension benefits. But the precise magnitude of the economic burden which the community as a whole should bear is a matter of current controversy. The matter is complicated by the fact that although many elderly persons are in the labor force because they find positive values in work itself, others are working mainly for the income to be derived from it. Because this is so, the total cost of increased pension benefits would tend to rise more than in proportion to the rise in benefit rates, since many of those whose main motive for working is income would be induced to retire. Just how many of those now working would leave the work force in response to a (say) 25 per cent rise in retirement income (from public or private sources) cannot be estimated at present but here, at least, is the kind of calculation which must underlie policy-making in this sphere. And as, in the future, in response to health and medical improvements, the proportion of able elderly rises, the question will grow in importance.

What is the nature of the union's role in the decisions which govern the employment opportunity and the terms of retirement

---

single interest of the citizen tends to absorb him completely, then a threat to democratic institutions does exist." Lloyd H. Fisher, "The Politics of Age," in Milton Derber, editor, *The Aged and Society* (Champaign, Ill.: Industrial Relations Research Association, 1950), p. 165.

[4] See Sumner H. Slichter, "Retirement Age and Social Policy," in *ibid.*, pp. 106–114, from whom these terms have been borrowed; see also his "The Need for More Employment of Older Workers," *Wisconsin Labor 1951* (Wisconsin State Federation of Labor, 1951).

[5] See Robert Dorfman, "The Labor Force Status of Persons Aged Sixty-Five and Over," *American Economic Review*, XLIV (May, 1954). Dorfman, reporting on a Census survey, states that "77 per cent of the older men [over 64] who are not in the labor force feel that they are not well enough to work." *Ibid.*, p. 635.

offered older persons? Existing appraisals of trade union behavior toward the older worker cover a rather broad range. Although attention in recent years has focused mainly on the retirement question, union representatives appearing in panel discussions and conferences have also expressed the view that the older worker has the union to thank for considerably improving his employment prospects. This position has been most forcefully presented by Solomon Barkin:

> Over the years no group has been as continuously concerned with the problems of the older worker as the trade-unions. They have been vocal in protesting the fate of the qualified worker whose age group has been a handicap in getting employment; pioneers in the development of clauses in collective bargaining agreements protecting the worker's right to his job; and leaders in the battle for adequate financial provisions for the aged, both by private industry and the government.[6]

Barkin, in discussing a number of union practices whose effect is to improve the position of older workers, deals with the question at a rather general level; illustrative material is presented, but the author does not undertake to estimate the prevalence of specific policies or to discuss variations among unions in the vigor with which these policies are applied. Nor are union policies which may have an unfavorable impact upon the employment opportunity of older workers discussed.

The unfavorable policies are regarded more seriously by Albert J. Abrams whose focus has been upon the specific barriers to the employment of older persons which have been set up by unions, employers, government and older persons themselves. "The barriers imposed by unions to the hiring of older workers are largely of an indirect nature and have not been given thorough, critical analysis," Abrams states.[7] However, he lists a number which he feels clearly constitute "obstacles to the hiring of older workers." These include: reluctance of some unions to "open up entry jobs for older persons which would enable them to get a foothold in plants"; opposition of some unions to part-time work for retired

---

[6] See Solomon Barkin, "Union Policies and the Older Worker," in Milton Derber, editor, *The Aged and Society*, pp. 75–92.

[7] Albert J. Abrams, "Barriers to the Employment of Older Workers," in Clark Tibbitts, editor, *Social Contribution by the Aging* (Philadelphia: American Academy of Political and Social Science, 1952), p. 69.

members; operation of certain types of work permit systems; and "refusal of many unions to permit workers of declining abilities to be downgraded in pay or position."[8]

The view that unions are not loathe to eliminate the older workers from the labor market has been expressed by Sumner Slichter: "The majority of union members are young men who wish the older worker retired in order to create opportunities of promotion for the young men."[9] Also emphasizing the conflict of interests, Dunlop has referred to an "internal struggle over the locus of unemployment. The older workers will attempt to protect themselves by seniority, employees in favorably situated firms, departments, or occupations may attempt to pass the burden on."[10] And more recently, though in a somewhat different context, Stigler has observed, "Older workers will prefer retirement benefits where younger workers want current wage increases. One of the most striking developments in collective bargaining in recent years has been the triumph of the former over the latter."[11]

These comments raise a number of questions. Do the "favorable" union practices cited by Barkin and other union spokesmen outbalance the unfavorable effect of the "barriers" cited by Abrams and others? Is the net effect of unionism beneficial or harmful to the employment opportunity of the elderly worker? What governs the degree to which the young men who are "the majority of union members" will tolerate the presence of old men if, as Slichter suggests, the young men are anxious to see the old men retired? If the employer is also anxious to see the old men out of the work force, to what dgree will the union cooperate in helping him eliminate his older employees? How is union resistance to compulsory retirement explained where it occurs? How is union support of the same policy to be understood? And how, indeed, to repeat

---

[8] These findings were based in part on the responses to questionnaires and letters of a large number of labor organizations. The more complete report upon these responses is found in an earlier article by Albert J. Abrams, "Unions and the Older Worker," in No Time to Grow Old (Albany, New York: New York State Joint Legislative Committee on Problems of the Aging, 1951), pp. 119–144.

[9] See Slichter, "Retirement Age and Social Policy," p. 109.

[10] John T. Dunlop, Wage Determination under Trade Unions (New York: A. M. Kelley, 1950), pp. 36–37; see also Harry D. Wolf, "Railroads," in How Collective Bargaining Works (New York: The Twentieth Century Fund, 1942), pp. 355–356.

[11] George Stigler, The Theory of Price (New York: Macmillan, 1952), pp. 254–255.

Stigler's question, can we explain why such a high proportion of the money worth of the "packages" currently won in collective bargaining is set aside for retirement benefits?

The present investigation was an effort to gather information relevant to these questions through a review of union practices in a number of spheres in which the employment fate of the older worker is substantially determined. These include hiring, layoff, discharge, wage adjustment and, of course, pensions and retirement programs. A dozen major unions in the San Francisco Bay area were selected for study. These unions bargain for approximately 100,000 workers in the following major industry groups: manufacturing, construction, wholesale and retail trade, service, transportation, communications and public utilities. Thus, a relatively diverse industrial representation was obtained. The selection was made so that half of the unions chosen exerted some appreciable control over hiring procedures. In addition, an effort was made to secure some variety in connection with pension experience. For the rest, the selection was approximately random— perhaps "indifferent" would express it more accurately—though the factor of accessibility entered to some degree.

The survey was conducted mainly through personal interview with union officials. These officials were distributed throughout the union hierarchy; there were some international officers, international representatives, business agents, local officials and in several cases research directors, dispatchers and stewards. Coverage was not uniform but in only a small minority of cases were less than three union officials interviewed for each union. Moreover, the majority of officials were interviewed at least twice, and there were some with whom discussions were held on three or four occasions. The discussions with union officials were supplemented by a substantial but smaller number of talks with the employer representatives with whom the union officials customarily deal. Beyond this, study was given union and employer publications and other sources of information bearing directly on union policies in the selected labor markets.

Briefly, the principal object of the study was to identify the union policies mainly relevant to the position of older workers, and to isolate some of the important influences operative in the formation of these policies. In addition, although the methods used in the study permit no quantitative estimates of the impact of specific policies or of unionism as a whole on the employment opportunity of older persons,[12] a number of strong impressions concerning the direction of the impact emerged from the investigation, and these are offered below. The findings of the study are summarized at the end of Parts I and II, but it is well at this point to emphasize some of the qualifications to which they are subject. First, the scope was limited to the collective bargaining context. For example, no attempt was made to cover the legislative activity of unions. Secondly, something was lost from the fact that the investigation was conducted mainly at the level of the local unions whereas in many important matters critical decisions are made at the international level in response to pressures emerging mainly at that level. (An attempt was made to extend the boundaries of

---

[12] An effort to test statistically the impact of union policies on the employment opportunity of older workers would run into a number of difficulties. One might, for example, try to compare employment opportunity in predominately unionized and predominately non-unionized situations. (Estimates so derived would apply to the question addressed by Barkin and others concerning the total impact of unions on the position of older workers in given labor markets.) But available measures of the "extent of unionism" in various labor markets are notoriously blunt instruments. And similar difficulties are faced in the definition of a suitable index of employment opportunity. Associations of employment status with age—Census data give number of employed persons and "experienced workers seeking work" by age groups for each Census occupation and industry classification—and associations of age with earnings or days of employment over some specified time period are deficient for present purposes because labor markets offering poor employment opportunity to older workers induce their exit whereas those offering relatively favorable employment opportunity attract or hold them. (However, see Otto Pollak's "Discrimination Against Older Workers in Industry," *American Journal of Sociology*, (September, 1944), 99–106, in which use is made of 1930 and 1940 Census data of this kind in support of the contention that there has been a general inclination to overstate the problem of age discrimination. See also Stanley Lebergott's challenge of the Pollak position, *ibid.*, LI (January, 1946), 322–324, which, however, is based on grounds different from those just mentioned.) Another possibility is a simple comparison of age distributions. A figure such as the percentage of employed persons over 45 or over 65 years of age might serve as a rough index of the degree to which older persons are welcome or can be carried or accommodated in the various labor markets. But the chief difficulty here is that there are too many influences, apart from union policy, which have important impact. Chief among these, probably, is the nature of the occupational structure. Different degrees of required speed, agility, strength or skill will account for considerable variation in age composition. Age composition may differ markedly with variations in employer policy and the size of available pension benefits. On the whole, the available data are too gross to permit a satisfactory measure of the effect of union policy on the employment opportunity of older workers.

the study where necessary and where it was possible to do so.) Other limitations attach to the limited time period within which the field work was carried on. The study was, on the whole, primarily exploratory in nature; its findings are put forward not as conclusions throught to be definitive in any sense but rather as hypotheses urgently in need of further refinement.

PART I

# EMPLOYMENT OPPORTUNITY

## HIRING AND ENTRANCE

In some labor markets,[13] a strong control in the sphere of hiring represents a *sine qua non* of effective union operation. To insure its own survival, the union must abridge the discretionary authority of employers; otherwise, discrimination on the basis of union affiliation exists as an overwhelmingly powerful threat. This is especially true where employment is intermittent so that the individual worker is "hired" dozens or even hundreds of times in the course of maintaining something approaching regular employment over any considerable period of time.

The mechanisms instituted by unions to distribute work—some will be reviewed in detail below—are nearly always based on some variation of the principle of "first in, first out"; these are essentially nondiscriminatory in nature, that is, they do not permit discrimination on the basis of normal variations in competence nor do they permit discrimination on the basis of age.

The essence of the older worker's employment difficulty is that he is in competition for available jobs with other workers who, for a number of reasons, appear to be preferred over him by the

---

[13] The term "labor market" is used in this study to refer to the immediate economic environment within which the specific unions under observation customarily operate. In many cases the term "industry" might easily be substituted, but this term is no less ambiguous than the other. See the discussion of the "institutional labor market" in Clark Kerr, "Labor Markets: Their Character and Consequences," *American Economic Review*, XL (May, 1950), 282–283; also Clark Kerr, "The Balkanization of Labor Markets," in *Labor Mobility and Economic Opportunity* (The Technology Press of the Massachusetts Institute of Technology, 1954), pp. 93 ff.

employers. The basic benefit conferred on the older worker by the union-controlled placement procedures is protection from competition of this kind, through immunity from employer discrimination. The hiring mechanisms customarily narrow the grounds for rejection to competence to do the work. The critical contribution of the hiring control is that, especially with respect to competence, the burden of proof is now on the employer and not the individual workman. And this is likely to be of considerable significance. Employers are sometimes reluctant to hire older workers even if their competence is not in question, because it is believed that other costs, e.g., higher insurance rates, are associated with their employment. Under the rules governing the hiring of printers, longshoremen and sailors, as will be seen in the following sections, older workers are not subject to elimination for these reasons.

The key feature of the system of rules governing hiring in the typographical union's Bay Area jurisdictions is the near elimination not only of employer discretion but of the employer himself in the normal hiring process.

The power to hire is vested in the foreman in each shop. However, the foreman is a member of the union and there are some very practical limits to his authority. He may refuse to hire on the ground of incompetency but this decision is subject to review by the union, to which the rejected printer may appeal. As a result, the foreman is encouraged to intercede in what is almost an automatic hiring procedure only in relatively extreme situations.[14]

The set of rules governing hiring, besides limiting discretionary power of the employer to a minimum, permits printers, within some limits to select their own place of employment. Each shop of appreciable size has a crew of "regular situation" holders— guaranteed a five-day week by the employer—and a group of other printers who perform "extra work." The "extras" are needed for peak period operation and to fill in for regular employees who are on vacation or who are absent for any other reason. An out-

[14] The difficult position of the foreman who, acting as the representative of the employer, is at the same time subject to strong personal and formal restraints on the union side, was remarked upon by one union official who declared that the most populous occupational classification in the union is "ex-foreman."

of-work printer formally applies for a job simply by placing his name on the "slipboard" which is provided at any shop of appreciable size. He has "priority" at the shop, albeit the lowest in the shop, as soon as he has registered his name, and he is eligible for "extra work" in the order of this priority. As time passes, and vacancies appear, he is elevated to regular employment when his "priority" exceeds that of the other nonregular employees.

In longshoring, the policies governing hiring, though considerably different in form from those in printing, are very similar in impact.

The outstanding institution involved here is the hiring hall through which all longshore employment is channeled. In the San Francisco Bay Area where some 5,000 longshoremen are to be found, approximately 1,500 to 2,000 persons are dispatched each day to waterfront jobs. Although a substantial number of union members are attached to gangs and do not ordinarily go through the hiring hall, a good many men are likely to be "hired" two or three times during a single week. The governing principle in dispatching is that the person with the lowest number of hours worked receives the first claim on available work. The system, besides resulting in approximate equalization of employment among those regularly presenting themselves for work, has the additional feature of establishing an unambiguous standard for dispatching which again, as in printing, minimizes the element of decision normally present in the selection which has to be made among applicants for vacant jobs.

Thus, in longshoring as in printing the practical area of discretion remaining to the employer has been virtually eliminated. The longshoreman is dispatched from the hiring hall by one of the nine dispatchers, elected by the local's membership, and reports for work. Any interference with this process by an employer representative, as for example the rejection of a referent on the ground of incompetence, would represent a distinct departure from normal practice and would, except in extreme cases, be reviewed in the port grievance machinery.

A third union, the Sailors' Union of the Pacific, has instituted hiring procedures which are similar in impact to those just discussed. Here, as in longshoring, the hiring hall is the basic mechanism, and again the essential impact is that discretionary authority is reduced to a minimum. Sailors returning from voyages report to the hiring hall and receive a "shipping card" from the dispatcher. The hiring process consists simply of announcements by the dispatcher that jobs are available and the subsequent presentation of "shipping cards" by interested sailors in the hiring hall. Where two or more persons desire the same job, the man with the shipping card issued least recently has the prior claim.

As in printing and longshoring, the refusal of an employer to accept a sailor dispatched from the hiring hall would occasion an investigation by the union, and ultimately would necessitate some joint union-employer disposition of the case. The basic question of competence, however, is seldom raised in connection with age. Industry practice sanctions stiff medical examinations prior to voyages and sailors who pass this test are not likely to be challenged on the basis of ability to do the work.[15]

The hiring procedures just reviewed have been those of three unions which have secured a rather thoroughgoing control over the labor markets in which they operate. But the full extent of the benefit conferred on the older workers in these markets is not contained wholly in the operation of the basic placement mechanisms just described. The hiring controls place the unions in a position to institute supplementary policies which yield further advantages to the elderly in the respective labor markets.

Older workers among the printers are benefited by the working rule which permits them to hire "substitutes" if, for any reason, they choose not to report to work. The hire price is simply the wage for the day's work and the worker's obligation to the employer is fully discharged when he has engaged someone to take his place. As there is normally an adequate supply of extras attached to the larger shops, printers have considerable freedom to adjust their work to their physical and other needs. A printer wishing to work only three days per week for a substantial period of time may simply hire substitutes to fill out his regular work

---

[15] The union polices the examinations, as was revealed by a recent grievance. A rejected seaman had himself examined by a public health physician who declared him fit to work. The union's position—which finally prevailed—was that the opinion of a public health physician should take precedence over the findings of the physician of the employer.

week. A printer may be absent as much as ninety days in any twelve-month period "for pursuits other than at the trade" without loss of his priority standing; in cases of illness, however, his priority is protected for the whole period of his illness. And "illness" is liberally interpreted. "If a man says he's sick, he's sick," the president of the San Francisco local declared.

The longshore union has instituted a supplementary policy which favors its older members. It has established a category of "exempt" persons. These are members who have some physical disability so that they require extra consideration in dispatching. Applications for classification into this group are processed by a special investigating committee whose recommendations are reviewed by the local's executive board. The local has set aside one particular job classification (involving light work) for the benefit of the exempt personnel, and dispatchers are instructed to give exempt persons the lighter of other available jobs in the normal process of dispatching. One of the dispatchers estimated that "exempt" personnel account for about one per cent of current employment.

Not all of the work performed by members of the SUP is done at sea. A considerable amount of "standby work" is available to the union's members. This includes "shifting ship" (from one pier to another, for example) and painting, scraping and maintenance work of many kinds. This work, too, is subject to the "first in, first out" rule. However, an exception is made for the benefit of older workmen in the rules governing hiring procedures in one occupational classification. Coastwise Shipping Rule No. 18 reads, "Members fifty (50) years of age or over shall have preference for Watchmen's jobs only."[16]

The controls over hiring secured by other unions under investigation varied considerably in depth of penetration.[17] Those exercised by the machinists, warehousemen and building service

---

[16] According to the Dispatcher's Report for 1952, of the 14,693 jobs filled through the hiring hall in that year, only 16 were in the Watchman classification. An almost identical ratio prevailed in 1951.

[17] The control over hiring exercised by the Oakland electrical workers was nearly as complete in practice as some of those already discussed, while the control exercised by the San Francisco electrical workers was of a somewhat different order. Discussion of these two groups, however, is reserved for the latter part of this section.

workers ranged from moderately strong controls to situations in which only the mildest of preferences for union members could be discerned.

Contracts held by the machinists union customarily call for union shop and preferential hiring, and the various locals operate dispatching services. According to local officers, attempts are made to give preference in dispatching to members who have been out of work the longest, though it is necessary to devote considerable attention to relative qualifications of the available men. This is especially true where the preferential hiring provisions are somewhat tenous. A stipulation that the union ". . . shall have reasonable opportunity to refer applicants for the vacancies to be filled"[18] does not permit the kind of "first in, first out" dispatching procedures found on the waterfront or practices such as those of the printers. On the other hand, discrimination because of age has long been explicitly prohibited in the master contract between the union and the local employers council in the metal trades.[19]

The union's control over hiring in warehousing is considerably weaker than those so far discussed. The union's contract with the association of employers provides for a union shop and recognizes a hiring hall through which the applicants for vacancies in the principal occupations covered by the contract are to be channeled. Even so, the language of the contract provides considerable latitude for the employers.[20]

It should be noted that most jobs in warehousing are regular and likely to be held for long periods of time. The employers have insured their freedom to select their permanent employee force by a contract provision which exempts workers of less than 90 days service from the application of the seniority provisions. The employer is free to lay off any newly hired individual for any

[18] This particular language is found in the agreement between Marin County Lodge 238 and H. C. Little Burner Co.

[19] The provision in the Master Agreement between the California Metal Trades Association and the International Association of Machinsts simply states, "In hiring there shall be no age limit except as provided by law."

[20] The clause reads, "In the event the offices of the Union are unable within a reasonable time, to furnish competent and experienced men satisfactory to the Employer, the Employer may hire from outside sources." Agreement between the Distributors Association of Northern California and Warehouse Union Local 6, I. L. W. U.

[ 14 ]

reason during the first three months of his employment. The union's control over hiring is subject to very severe limitations, as a result.

The effect of union control of dispatching is to confront the employer with union-selected persons. The dispatcher does not pay any attention to age, but sends out the person who he feels can do the job in accordance with the system of rotation established by union policy. The hiring hall machinery cannot prevent employer discrimination on the basis of age insofar as additions to regular employee forces is concerned. But the employer is under pressure to give the dispatched persons a chance; if he rejects prior to giving the referent a chance at the job, the union complains.[21] Dispatching procedure operates on a system of priority which gives the first claim to a vacant job to the individual present in the hiring hall who has been out of work the longest time, provided however, that if the individual refuses this job he forfeits his claim and must go to the end of the line. Older workers, on the other hand, are permitted to keep their priority until jobs are available which they can fill. Thus the lighter jobs are in effect reserved for them. Of course, as noted above, the union is powerless to force employers to retain the elderly for any considerable length of time.

Union control over hiring approaches the vanishing point in some of the labor markets represented by the building service workers; employer discretion is almost complete. Locals of the union maintain dispatching halls, but the union control over hiring consists mainly of the fact that for most employers it is more convenient to hire through the union than it is to solicit help from outside sources. Although contracts held by some locals are somewhat more favorable to the union, a typical contract provision reads as follows:[22]

When vacancies occur in positions subject to this Agreement, the Employer shall notify the Union office and shall afford it an opportunity to send applicants for the position. The Employer may likewise consider other applicants for the position who may or may not be

---

[21] One of the local's business agents appeared ready to enter a complaint in one instance when 60 men had to be dispatched to fill 34 vacancies.

[22] Master Agreement between the San Francisco Hospital Conference and Hospital and Institutional Workers' Union, Local 250-AFL, 1952–1955, p. 10.

members of the Union. The Employer may employ the person who, in his judgment, will make the best employee. The Employer shall be the sole judge of the fitness of any applicant.

Faced with such contract provisions, the union is considerably limited in its dispatching policy with the result that, in order to retain its function as supplier of labor to the employers, the union is likely to send out the applicant who has the best chance of satisfying the employer. In Oakland, it is not unusual for the union to dispatch several applicants simultaneously for a single opening. It is up to the individual applicant to "sell himself to the employer," to use a local officer's expression.

The foregoing indicates that the degree of protection in hiring conferred upon the elderly union member is likely to vary directly with the degree to which the union has managed to secure control over the labor market. But the same does not apply to older workers who do not already have a claim upon the union for protection. To them it is likely to make little difference whether the employer or the union controls the hiring mechanism; they are often discriminated against in either case.

In a number of labor markets under investigation in the present study, hiring was essentially an employer prerogative. This was the case in oil refining, electric and gas utilities, steel, automobiles, and telephones—industries in which employment if not generally steady is at least not intermittent as in many craft occupations or as in shipping and longshoring. As a consequence union pressures for control over the hiring mechanism have been largely negligible. Age discrimination in hiring new employees is practiced by most of the employers in these industries. In many cases it is virtually impossible for workers approaching 35, not to mention those older, to break through the employment barriers. The unions have been generally indifferent to these practices. It is true that from time to time, representatives of the labor groups involved—mainly officers or staff representatives at the international level—have publically deplored age discrimination in hiring, but there was little evidence in the present study of serious efforts to apply pressure to the employers on this issue. In no case had union objections reached the point at which the matter had entered contract negotiations, nor was there evidence of pressure through grievance procedures. For the most part local officials were not appreciably provoked by the company hiring practices.

Among the unions covered in the present study, those which have secured the most complete control over hiring procedures also enforced strict controls over entry into their respective labor markets. In each case, barriers had been established against the entry of elderly persons.

The typographical union administers an apprenticeship program through which the largest portion of entrants into the local market is channeled. A number enter as transferred members from other areas, and full membership rights are automatically conferred on these transferees. A few may enter on the basis of experience gained in nonunion shops, but these are subjected to rigid examination, and entry is not easily achieved in this manner. The main port of entry is through the apprenticeship program. And only young men are admitted to this program.

Entry in longshoring occurs through registration at the hiring hall. But registration is supervised by a joint union-employer committee and each party has an effective veto. During the course of the present investigation, registration in San Francisco was closed so that there was no entry at all. Elsewhere a precedent has been set to give younger applicants preference. When one of the smaller Northern ports was opened not long ago, an age limit of 40 years was instituted.

Entry into the sailors' union is effected through graduation from the Andrew Furuseth School. This training school is operated by the union and according to one union official, men beyond their thirties are not encouraged to enter. When employment opportunities are scarce, enrollment in the school may be stopped entirely.

The machinists' union insists on contract provisions which prohibit discrimination against its members solely on the basis of age, in hiring. Yet the union sponsors an apprentice program which bars entry to anyone over the age of 23.

Lack of concern over employer discrimination against nonmember older workers and active union discrimination in the cases just cited are not, of course, incompatible with the policies reviewed earlier. If union members are not involved, internal political implications of discrimination are largely absent. Nor is the discrimination a threat to union security for the usual reasons. In fact, the stiff entrance policies may be traceable in part to a community of interest between union and employer: preservation of the quality of the work force. This may appear to imply inverse relationship between age and efficiency which, as extensive research in recent years has clearly shown, cannot be lightly assumed. But—especially if we think of older workers as those approaching the conventional retirement age—in those labor markets in which speed and strength are of special importance the proposition is not so shaky. Moreover, unions may find it profitable to act as if age and efficiency were inversely related, if only because their bargaining partners, the employers, believe that they are, or prefer younger workers for other reasons. It is considerations of just this sort which partly set the limits to the amount of supplementary protection which unions choose to confer on their older members. All of these relationships are particularly well defined in the cases of the San Francisco and Oakland electrical workers, a discussion of which follows.

Local 6 (San Francisco) and Local 595 (Oakland) of the International Brotherhood of Electrical Workers are known as "building trades" locals because important segments of their memberships are employed in the construction industry. Each local holds a master contract with the association of electrical contractors in its respective community as well as a number of other contracts, among which are those covering work in marine, neon sign, and "motor" shops. Some 1,000 of the approximately 2,200 members of Local 6 and some 600 of the 1,400 members of Local 595 are typically engaged in construction, according to estimates given by the two locals' business managers. The essential similarity of the two locals extends to the industrial distribution of the remainder of the membership as well.[3] Both locals operate in what amounts to effective closed shop situations and the work-

---

[3] The next most numerous group of workers in both locals are those in marine work. These were estimated at some 400 for Local 6 and some 250 for Local 595.

ing rules and conditions on both sides of the Bay are not greatly different from each other. But a major exception to this pattern lies in the hiring procedures adopted by the two locals.

The rule in Local 595 (Oakland) is that all hiring be carried on through the union. Employers with job vacancies notify the union, which dispatches the required number of men. This hiring system confers on the union considerable latitude in its dealings with individual contractors, whom in extreme situations it could favor or discipline through variations in the competency of the workmen dispatched. Since the industry is one in which labor costs constitute a large fraction of total costs this is an important instrument of power. The basic rule in dispatching, according to the local's business manager, is that the vacant jobs go to the most competent men, with the proviso, however, that length of time out of work is an important though not the ruling factor in selection. Supplementary policy thus reserves the lighter work for older men who require it, and certain very light jobs such as equipment handling and distribution are set aside for the superannuated and partially disabled.

Actually, it is the local's strategic control over hiring which lies at the center of the basic relationship prevailing between the union and the employers' association. The union possesses an ultimate threat of striking the local contractors while inviting outside contractors into the area with the promise of high-quality labor. Of course there are certain degrees with which this sanction can be imposed. As a matter of basic policy, the union has kept a number of local contractors out of the local contractors' association for just such bargaining purposes, and apparently with appreciable success. The union's divisive policy has contributed to a situation characterized by the local contractors as oppressively competitive, however. Some of the implications of this for the union's policy toward older workers in another sphere will be explored shortly.

In San Francisco electrical workers are permitted to solicit employment, although the union operates a dispatching service for employers who wish to hire through the union and for members who either cannot or do not wish to seek work directly from employers. The local's business manager estimates that about half of the hiring is done through the union dispatcher. One result of the policy of permitting soliciting by members is a keen competition for work. For, with wages fixed by contract, income depends on the steadiness of employment, and the likelihood of steady work is enhanced if the individual establishes a reputation as a good fast worker.

The relationship between the union and the contractor's association is considerably more harmonious in San Francisco than it is in Oakland. In fact, two San Francisco employers who were interviewed described the union as "very cooperative." The prevailing good will can be traced apparently to a number of factors of which three major ones are listed here.

1. The hiring procedures just described offer strong incentives for worker efficiency, as was noted above. And an additional reason for relatively high efficiency is the fact that employers are permitted to build up stable employee forces which remain with them for long periods of time. One contractor with operations in both San Francisco and Oakland stated that his unit labor costs are customarily estimated to be nearly 10 per cent higher in Oakland than in San Francisco.

2. The San Francisco local does not follow the divisive policy practiced in Oakland. In fact, Local 6 is more likely to discourage than it is to encourage the intrusion of outside contractors.[24] Although it is impossible to evaluate the extent to which this policy is pursued, the general effect at least, is to shelter rather than to "spoil" the market.

3. Local 6 accepts the principle of "job protection" which means that when wage increases through collective bargaining are instituted, these new rates do not apply to projects which were begun before the effective date of the wage increase. The Oakland local on the other hand insists that wage increases apply to all electrical work as soon as they are officially instituted.

Do the older electricians in the San Francisco local fare any

[24] This was corroborated in interviews with both employer and union representatives in Oakland and San Francisco, though there were differences in the degree of importance attributed to it. One informant characterized operations in the two communities as follows: "In San Francisco the union members compete against each other, while in Oakland the contractors have to compete." A San Francisco employer said: "We don't have the high fence of the old days any more. Local contractors might get a little preference in quality of the men, though."

worse than their brethren in Oakland? From a bare account of the two hiring mechanisms one might be led to suppose that they do. For in Oakland where there is somewhat greater emphasis on employment equalization, each employer is more or less compelled to absorb his share of slower older men. But it is a consequence of the type of hiring procedures in San Francisco that

TABLE I

AGE DISTRIBUTION OF MEMBERS OF THE INTERNATIONAL BROTHERHOOD OF ELECTRICAL WORKERS, LOCALS 595 AND 6
February, 1953

| Age Group | Local 595 | | Local 6 | |
|---|---|---|---|---|
| | Number | Per cent | Number | Per cent |
| Less than 35 years. | 383 | 27.6 | 551 | 25.4 |
| 35–44 years. | 365 | 26.2 | 605 | 28.0 |
| 45–54 years. | 386 | 27.8 | 613 | 28.3 |
| 55–64 years. | 231 | 16.6 | 347 | 16.0 |
| 65 and older. | 24 | 1.7 | 48 | 2.2 |
| Total. | 1,389 | 99.9[a] | 2,164 | 99.9[a] |

SOURCE: International Brotherhood of Electrical Workers, Washington, D.C.
[a] Percentages do not add to 100.0 because of rounding.

the slowest and least efficient have the most difficulty in maintaining employment. As a result of this, the older electricians make disproportionate use of the union's dispatching service. It was, as a matter of fact, in corroboration of his statement that "the old guy works when everybody works" and the judgment that, in general, the older electrical workers secure less employment than the others that the local's business manager cited the relatively high age of the group characteristically patronizing the dispatching service. He also noted the presence of a vocal older group which complains of the pace set by the younger "eager beavers."

But it would be a mistake to jump to the conclusion that the older union men fare appreciably worse in San Francisco than in Oakland. At least, the available statistics of the age distribution of the membership in the two jurisdictions show no important differences between the two. These data, shown in Table I, indicate, rather a surprising similarity.

This age distribution comparison, though it is free of the many defects attaching to such comparisons between heterogeneous groups of workers,[25] may not be an adequate index of employment opportunity in the present case for two reasons: (a) the data refer to a period during which employment levels were relatively high and may not be representative of periods when the competition for work is more intense; (b) members include many electricians who are no longer working at the trade or who are employed only intermittently but who maintain membership in order to retain eligibility for the pension. It is entirely possible that the older members in one area are getting relatively less work than those in the other. But the supplementary data to verify this possibility are not available.

Just the same, the similarities in age distributions are very impressive. As a matter of fact, there is some positive evidence that despite the relatively inferior position in which the elderly San Francisco union member is placed by the institution of competition in the hiring mechanism, his situation is alleviated by a semi-formal understanding that the employers are to "take care of" the older workers among the membership, though this is sometimes accomplished only after some supplementary cajolery by the local's business manager.

The contracts held by both local unions contain provisions that a fifth of the journeymen employed must be 55 years of age or older. But these clauses are not rigidly enforced. The business manager of the San Francisco local said: "It's on paper all right, but it's pretty hard to force contractors to keep the old guys." One San Francisco contractor declared that he has never heard of its being rigidly applied. Because contract clauses of this type are invariably mentioned in discussions of union policy toward the older worker, it is interesting to note in the two locals under study that the clauses are not enforced with the same kind of mathematical rigor in which they are expressed. The clauses stand rather as statements of principle to which the union is able to refer from time to time; no one is charged with the task of keeping a running census of employment and age distribution. As a result, the frequency with which the provision is invoked will depend

---

[25] See footnote 12.

to a great degree on how vocal the older members are and on the degree of interest in enforcing the provision evidenced by the union officers. The latter, of course, are under constant pressure from the employers as well as the older workers.

It is apparently in the sphere of entrance that the ultimate effect of the Oakland local's insistence on control of hiring is felt.

Both Local 6 and Local 595 pursue restrictive admission policies. In addition to regulating the number of apprentices entering annually, the locals limit the number of "travelers" who are permitted to attain full membership rights.[26] The rest of the travelers are granted work permits. This status is an inferior one because of the rule enforced by both locals that permit men are not to be given work while full members of the union are unemployed. These restrictions on entry are familiar ones in the building trades and they are especially familiar in the electrical workers' unions. What is worth noting, however, is that the Oakland local has adopted a conscious policy of improving the quality of its work force through use of its entrance control. For it would appear that resistance of Oakland employers to Local 595 wage demands in contract negotiations has made the union acutely efficiency conscious and thus concerned with the level of competence of its membership. And this in turn has resulted in selection of an entrance policy with a definite accent on youth.

In contrast to the relatively peaceful bargaining relations between union and employers in San Francisco—there has been no strike since 1921—the Oakland relationship has been one of conflict. As a general rule, the Oakland local has had to fight for concessions granted without a battle to Local 6. Local 595 had to strike twice, for example, to attain a vacation plan which had been secured by the San Francisco local without evidence of conflict.

The complaint most frequently heard by Local 595 negotiators is that "productivity" is poor. The Oakland contractors argue forcefully that the procedures established by Local 595 yield a level of performance which does not warrant wage-and-conditions parity with San Francisco where employers have the benefit

---

[26] Union officials explain that the long construction season and other desirable features make the Bay Area a very choice region, so that "tough" entrance policies are necessary to prevent a too-heavy influx of electricians from other parts of the country.

of greater freedom in the labor market and as a result, it is said, higher labor productivity.[27] But the union insists on parity as a fundamental point of policy. And it has responded with an entrance policy aimed at improving worker efficiency. Specifically, the local is expanding its membership through the apprentice program rather than through the admission of permit men who have been attached to the local for considerable periods of time.[28] This method is preferred because efficiency in the industry is associated not only with the speed and agility of youth, but also because the modern apprenticeship training program equips graduates with more technical competency and versatility than many of the older permit men are likely to possess.[29] At the time of the present study, plans called for the entry of some 20 new apprentices per year for the next several years. This was well in excess of the number of Local 595 members retiring on pension annually. An increasing volume of work in Alameda County requires a portion of the increased membership, but the rest will probably enter at the expense of employment currently going to older permit men. Even if no permit men are forced out of the trade under present conditions, any future overall curtailment in employment would bring on their exit at an increased rate as a result of the present intake of new members, who would have priority in employment.

The local's business manager estimated that the program would bring about a reduction in the average age of electricians engaged in construction by some five years. He ventured the opinion that the resulting higher efficiency of the work force would be expressed ultimately in higher wages and better working conditions.

---

[27] See, for example, Sumner H. Slichter, *Union Policies and Industrial Management* (Washington: The Brookings Institution, 1941), p. 86, where it is noted that "union control of hiring is likely to be partcularly disastrous to efficiency in the building trades."

[28] A few permit men are being admitted to membership. It was stressed repeatedly that the criteria of selection in such instances are "competency" and demonstrated capacity to uphold "union principles."

[29] There are, of course, a number of exceptions to this rule. In fact, a complaint made by the employers is that a number of apprentices who have been chosen because they are the sons of electrical workers seem to feel that their parentage and not their competency justifies their existence in the trade.

## LAYOFFS

Control over layoffs is sought for the same important reasons for which the controls over hiring are sought: job security for individual union members and security for the organization against discriminatory discharge. But the mechanism which is most usually instituted to effect this control—seniority—confers a greater measure of protection upon older workers than the analogous devices which are usually instituted to enforce union controls in the sphere of hiring.

A seniority system introduces a tangible and relatively unambiguous criterion, the effect of which is to reduce employer discriminations against older workers on the basis of minor differences in competence or for other reasons associated with their age. A seniority system also shifts the burden of proof to the employer, but it goes even further than that; it discriminates in *favor* of the older workers.[30]

Although seniority provisions covering layoffs are to be found in the vast majority of union contracts, and though the principle of seniority has come to be identified as one of the central principles of trade unionism, itself, it remains a subject of lively controversy, not only in connection with disputes between unions and employers, but also in connection with internal problems arising from differences among the membership over its appropriate scope and application. In fact, the basic differences over the principle are very similar to those reviewed earlier in the case of hiring control.

The union's dispute with the employer is most usually over the extent to which seniority relative to other standards ("ability," "fitness," etc.) shall rule in the selection of individual workers for layoff. Since part of the union's insistence on seniority as the ruling consideration in this sphere can be attributed to the desire to protect the job security of long-service workers, the older worker is thus a direct beneficiary of the policy. For this positive benefit, of course, the entire membership may have to "pay" in terms of employer resistance or ill-will and the consequences which flow from them. Thus the possibility of compromise involving more or less

[30] Workers with the greatest seniority are not always the oldest workers but the association is close enough to warrant discussion of the seniority principle as one of the primary union policies affecting the older worker.

[ 25 ]

protection to elderly workers in exchange for concessions in other spheres is always present. But the older worker has less to fear from this prospect precisely because of the other ends which are served simultaneously by the principle of seniority. The leading consideration is, of course, union security, as was mentioned above, but there are others: elimination of petty favoritism on the part of foremen, reduction in the pressure for speed-up in the pace of work, and so on.[31] Thus the older worker receives a large measure of his protection as a by-product of the union's endeavor to secure itself and to eliminate certain undesired practices.

A somewhat different set of considerations exists in connection with the second area of decision, that involving the internal aspects of the seniority question. To what degree is the job security of the older union members to be protected at the expense of that of the younger members. Two questions are of relevance here. The first concerns the choice between laying off the shorter service men and sharing the reduced quantity of employment among the entire group, young and old.[32] The interest of the older worker is best served by the former policy, but his job security is not really at stake even if the latter is selected. The second question is more serious for the older worker. It has to do with the scope of his seniority rights; i.e., with the appropriate unit within which his seniority shall apply: "occupational group," "department," "plant," or "company." The less inclusive the area of application of seniority, the greater is the vulnerability of the older worker to displacement and eventual loss of employment opportunity.[33]

The divisive implications of seniority and the compromise nature of the policy in this sphere which emerges from each union have been generally recognized in the literature.[34] It is particularly

[31] See Slichter, op. cit., Chapter IV, for a more complete catalog of union motives to control layoffs.

[32] The employer may or may not have a strong preference in this sphere in the case of moderately large movements in either direction.

[33] As substantial costs are often involved in the administration of a seniority system in which the area of application of seniority rights is very broad, e.g., in "plant seniority," the position of the employer on this question may enter as a primary force in the ultimate decision.

[34] See especially F. Harbison, "Seniority in Mass Producing Industries," *Journal of Political Economy*, XLVIII (December, 1940), 851–864; Slichter, *Union Policies and Industrial Management*, pp. 112, 156–157; *How Collective Bargaining Works* (New York: The Twentieth Century Fund, 1942), pp. 149, 355–356, 554, 659. See

in connection with this question that Harbison's speculation of a decade and a half ago is of especial interest. The proposition is that with the passage of time and the successful institutionalization of itself in the labor market a trade union's policy toward seniority will undergo change. For if the union no longer has to fear employer attacks on its right to exist, there will be less need to insist on strict versions of seniority for the "union security" reasons mentioned above.[35] The union may be less impelled, therefore, to oppose the employer in the more extreme instances in which differences in "ability" or "fitness" can be clearly discerned. Thus the union's willingness to extend protection to the older member whose abilities are failing may diminish as its own security improves. A second speculation leads to a similar hypothesis. As, with the passage of time, grievances which figured importantly in the early days of unionization have been dissipated and employers have moderated practices which inspired employee antagonism, the union may experience greater difficulty in holding the loyalty of its members. This difficulty may be especially pronounced in the case of the younger and newer workers who have little knowledge of pre-union conditions and who are not greatly impressed with the contribution which the union makes to them currently in exchange for their dues payments. The union leadership, in this case, in the interest of greater internal solidarity, may be less inclined to sponsor the more inclusive units of seniority application and more inclined to choose work sharing over layoffs. Thus in the case of the "internal" decision, the position of the older worker may be regarded with somewhat less solicitude as the union organization matures. These hypotheses suggest, in sum, that present policies toward seniority are still very much in the process of evolution and hence may be subject to substantial revision in any period in which unemployment is severe enough to inspire serious internal or external pressures.

A number of unions covered in the present survey were affected to a substantial degree by the decline in employment beginning in the last half of 1953 but, for the most part, the un-

---

also Leonard R. Sayles, "Seniority: An Internal Union Problem," *Harvard Business Review*, XXX (January–February), 1952), 55–61.

[35] Harbison, *op. cit.*, pp. 861–862.

employment problem had not reached a point at which severe strain was put on the established mechanisms for dealing with it. Nevertheless, there have been significant developments in a few instances.

Of all the unions covered in the present survey, the most acute unemployment situation in the postwar period has been faced by the longshore workers union. The experience of that organization illustrates most graphically the highly divisive character of disputes in which seniority is a central issue. The plight of the union in the early postwar years has been most revealingly discussed by Kerr and Fisher, who have gone so far as to attribute to the unusually severe unemployment problem with which the union was faced a major role in the transformation of the relationship between the union and the waterfront employers.[36] That relationship had been one of open warfare dating back to the San Francisco general strike of 1934 out of which the ILWU emerged as a going concern and which, as a matter of fact, the union's own efforts at organization and recognition occasioned. But with the conclusion of a particularly bitter and paralyzing 95-day strike at the end of 1948, a new kind of relationship seems to have been accepted, and since that time negotiations have been conducted without benefit of the strikes, lockouts and the other forms of conflict to which members of the industry had grown accustomed. Kerr and Fisher cite competitive pressures as the leading spur to a revision of employer attitudes. The employers hoped that improved efficiency and fewer stoppages would arise from friendlier relations with the union. The authors, in searching for an explanation of the change in the union attitude, comment, after reviewing a number of alternative explanations:[37]

A more credible explanation is the unemployment hypothesis. Longshore employment has declined seriously below wartime levels in all Pacific Coast ports. . . . Unemployment has always been a specially difficult problem for the longshore locals of the ILWU because of the large measure of control the union exercises over who shall be employed in the industry. With union control over the hiring hall and a system of work equalization through rotary dispatch, the available

---

[36] Clark Kerr and Lloyd Fisher, "Conflict on the Waterfront," *Atlantic Monthly*, 184 (September, 1949), 17–23.
[37] *ibid.*, pp. 21–22.

work opportunities are divided evenly among the registered long-shoremen. When aggregate unemployment declines seriously, all long-shoremen are underemployed.... The more conciliatory mood of the ILWU was doubtless in part a response to the press of unemployment within its ranks, and a desire to improve the employment opportunities of the longshore working force.

The great wave of unemployment among the longshoremen resulting from the abrupt drop in the quantity of cargo moving through West Coast ports after World War II was particularly severe in the San Francisco area. The local union responded to the slackening of work with the "deregistration" of short service men. "In conformity with the provisions adopted during the war to drop new members on a seniority basis, eight hundred men were dropped from the membership list in 1945."[38]

Although this action reduced the severity of the problem it did not eliminate it; underemployment persisted until the outbreak of the Korean War in 1950. An internal crisis in the affairs of the San Francisco local developed, moreover, when the conflicting interests over employment became entangled with longer standing internal problems. The deregistration issue became a focus not only for discord between high and low seniority men but also for conflicts arising out of racial—many of the men who faced possible deregistration were Negroes who had entered the industry during World War II—and even ideological differences. Proposals for and opposition to deregistration became important parts of the platforms of the factions opposing each other in campaigns for office in the local union.

In 1948 and again in 1949, the conflicts were brought to a head when specific proposals for deregistration were put to membership vote. In January 1948, the motion before the membership was for the elimination of 500 of the low-seniority men. It was defeated. Again in May 1949—San Francisco longshoremen were averaging about 25 hours of work per week in this period—a deregistration proposal was brought forward, this time aiming at the layoff of 800 men. It, too, was defeated after a vigorous battle.

In the following year, the onset of the Korean War brought a

---

[38] Wayne Wilbur Hield, *Democracy and Oligarchy in the International Longshoremen's and Warehousemen's Union* (M.A. dissertation, University of California, 1952), p. 197.

great increase in traffic through the San Francisco port with the result that the employment picture brightened considerably. Since that time, there has been no recurrence of severe unemployment difficulties. In any case, the union's experience clearly illustrates the divisive aspects of seniority and the difficulties which may arise when the principle is invoked to deal with a serious shortage of employment opportunity. As is suggested at a later point, the harrowing experience of five years of internal disturbance centering about unemployment may have been one of the important factors behind the union leadership's strongly favorable disposition toward the institution of a liberal retirement program.

With the onset of the general decline in business activity in the last half of 1953, several locals representing workers in oil refineries in the Bay area experienced a drop in employment and there were some layoffs in accordance with contract provisions of very long standing. Although the problem of unemployment was not a severe one locally, there were some other areas in the country, particularly in the East, in which unemployment was substantial, and this, together with the long run threat of technological employment, was sufficient to evoke a great deal of discussion among union officials.

The Oil Workers International Union favored a reduction of hours of work as the appropriate response to unemployment. There was a 36-hour work week in the oil refining industry during the depression of the thirties, but the work week was changed to 40 hours with the coming of World War II. The 40-hour work week has persisted until the present time, although the union has, on occasion, sought to return to the prewar work schedule.

In September 1952, the convention of the Oil Workers International Union approved the report of the union's Policy Committee which endorsed the shorter work week, saying in part[39]

The future tide of prosperity in the nation is uncertain. There is a possibility that a recession may develop and many people may be unemployed. Rather than see a large number of oil workers unemployed, the 36-hour work week should be re-instituted in the oil industry when necessary. Negotiation of such stand-by clauses now will prevent the development of a bitter dispute on the subject at a later date.

[39] *Proceedings*, Oil Workers International Union Convention (September 1–5, 1952), p. 54.

A year later, the union's convention unanimously endorsed a special resolution supporting the 36-hour work week which urged "all bargaining groups . . . to intensify their efforts to secure stand-by clauses in their contracts providing for a return to the 36-hour work week in case of serious unemployment nationally or sharp reductions in work forces locally. . . ."[40]

Local officials interviewed in the course of the present study reiterated the position of the international union in favor of a reduction in the length of the work week as a response to unemployment in preference to layoffs to meet the problem. One official declared that one of the advantages of dividing available work among the work force was that it enabled the workers in the lower-paid skills to perform some of the higher-paid work and thus recover some of the income lost due to the reduction in hours worked.

If there was a division of opinion among the membership in the Bay area locals on the subject of layoffs vs. part-timing it was not disclosed by the local officials. It is quite possible in this case that the relatively mild incidence of unemployment in the Bay area refineries had occasioned no great internal divisions. But that there were differences of opinion of a very serious nature within the industry on this issue seems clear from the comments of the international union's president, O. A. Knight, who in addressing the 1953 Convention said, in part:[41]

I know that it is extremely difficult to sell our people on the 36-hour work week. I know their thinking. Our program, of course, as adopted last year, calls for the 36-hour work week without a reduction in the take-home pay, and that would necessitate an increase in the hourly rates. But workers know that when you get launched on these programs, even though you might get consent on the part of the employer, get agreement from him to reduce the hours of work, it takes a hard battle to get him to do so with enough increase in the basic rates of pay to bring about a continuance of present take-home pay. . . .

So the fight must be on the basis of a 36-hour work week with full take-home pay. . . . Now why do we have difficulty in selling this to our members? As I have said, first of all, they don't know for sure that they are going to come out of it with the full take-home pay. But secondly, they look at it in another direction, too. I worked in a plant

[40] *Ibid.*, (September 28–October 2, 1953), p. 75.
[41] *Ibid.*, pp. 73–74.

during the last depression. . . . And I know that the layoffs in that plant did not run, even during the heart of the depression, more than thirty-three and a third per cent. So you've got a third of the people down on the bottom of the seniority list who are menaced, but you've got two-thirds up above who say, "Well, maybe I won't get laid off anyhow." And for that reason it is hard to sell to the majority of our membership that this sort of a program is mandatory.

This statement, together with the attitudes expressed by local union leadership indicates that the position of this union's leadership in the question of layoffs vs. part-timing is on the side of the latter program, at least in a situation in which unemployment threatens as a serious problem. This position places the incumbent leadership in alliance with the younger members who stand to lose their jobs in a period of declining employment. Of course, the degree to which the leadership is willing to press its program against the resistance of the long-service (older) members is a matter of conjecture. There is no real evidence, either, of the degree of resistance to part-timing which the high seniority group will offer. The experience in the oil refining industry is still too meager to offer much support for speculation along these lines.

It is a tribute to the explosiveness potential in the issue that the details of the application of seniority provisions in the collective bargaining agreements in a number of major industries are left to local determination. This is the situation in the steel industry, in which over 2,500 locals bargain local agreements on the application of seniority. The one large steel union local in the Bay region was handling its employment decline primarily through the layoff route, and the chief local official defended the policy largely through a defense of the seniority principle. Because only about five per cent of the regular members had been laid off by the spring of 1954, internal pressures for part-timing could hardly have had much of an opportunity to gain strength, even if they were potentially present. The Bay region steel local was, for this reason, scarcely representative of the industry, which was operating at about two-thirds of capacity.

The local official expressed another objection to work-sharing as a response to the unemployment problem. His sentiment was roughly as follows:

If you keep 4000 men to do the work of 2000 men, it is impossible to keep job borderlines from breaking down. This is the "speed up" problem in our industry. If you let an electrician do a welder's job, you find that the company begins to accommodate itself to this situation by assigning electricians with an hour or so on their hands to do an hour's worth of welding. Pretty soon, you look around and you find that five men who have acquired a whole lot of skills are doing the work of six. The union has fought for a long time to have jobs and the duties of each man carefully defined. The leadership is farseeing enough to recognize the value of this achievement and will not let the company nibble it away in a period of depression.

The official program of the United Steelworkers of America did not at this time include the proposal for a reduced work week. It rather endorsed the guaranteed annual wage and called for "enlightened action by government in the fields of social welfare, taxes, public works, housing and the advancement of farm security" in order to "bring this economic downturn to a quick end."[42] The union reported that on August 15, 1954, 211,678 of its nearly 1,200,000 members were totally unemployed and 188,233 were working less than a 40-hour week.[43]

Although the majority of the unions covered in the present study suffered some unemployment difficulties in the decline in activity which began in the last half of 1953, these were generally mild and short-term in nature. There was little evidence that substantial changes in the existing layoff procedures were in progress. It is clear, however, that none of the unions sees "seniority" in layoffs as a final principle in the sense of a solution to the problem of unemployment. The oil workers have their program for a shorter work week. The steelworkers and automobile workers ask for governmentally-sponsored full employment programs; meanwhile, they have sought and attained supplemental unemployment benefits. But paralleling these programs aimed at the alleviation of unemployment distress are programs for higher pension benefits which appear to embody a conscious effort to induce the older workers to retire. The traditional choice, layoff vs. part-timing,

---

[42] David J. McDonald, "Steelworkers and the National Economy," *Special Report to the 7th Constitutional Convention, United Steelworkers of America* September 20–24, 1954), p. 29.

[43] *Ibid.*, p. 5.

seems, to some degree at least, to have been transformed into layoff vs. pension off. The elaboration of this theme is left to the discussion of pension and retirement policies in Part II.

## WAGE AND OTHER ADJUSTMENTS

One of the most prominently mentioned "barriers" to the employment of older workers is the trade union policy of the standard rate. Marshall long ago criticized the "practice . . . of refusing to allow an elderly man, who can no longer do a full standard day's work, to take something less than standard wages" as one of "false standardization." He declared that: "It lowers the national dividend considerably: it condemns elderly men to take their choice between oppressive idleness, and a weary struggle to work harder than is good for them."[44] Henry Simons made a similar argument against the standard rate claiming that employment of the low grade workers was forfeited in the absence of commensurate wage concessions. In the old days, Simons argued, venturesome enterprises used to get a start by experimenting with low cost (albeit low grade) labor, and their contribution was to find better uses for existing labor relegated to low-value uses. Rigid application of the standard rate chokes off this kind of investment, Simons argued, and the employment associated with it.[45]

More recently, the absence of freely adjustable wage rates has been most seriously lamented by Sumner Slichter who has written that "failure to utilize more completely the productive capacity of the older workers in the community is one of the greatest wastes in modern history."[46] His remedy is to raise the normal retirement age and to adjust wage compensation to the abilities of the older workers through encouragement of the spread of piece work (which automatically adjusts wages to output). Where piece work could not be instituted, Slichter proposes a simple subsidy of employers who retain aged persons in their employee forces.

The remedies implicit in these suggestions operate through one of two channels. The first would improve the employment op-

[44] Alfred Marshall, *Principles of Economics* (8th ed.; London: Macmillan, 1920), pp. 707–708.

[45] Henry Simons, *Economic Policy for a Free Society* (Chicago: University of Chicago Press, 1948), pp. 139–140.

[46] Slichter, *Wisconsin Labor 1951*.

portunity of older workers through the increase in total employment. The second would improve their opportunity relative to all other workers.

The improvement via the route of greater total employment rests on the assumed efficacy of the classical recommendation of wage reduction. One must certainly be cautious in proffering this advice for the economy as a whole but it is quite possible that at the level of a particular industry the classical medicine would work. It would also seem, *a priori*, that the incidence of unemployment could be shifted away from the older person if he were allowed to offer special wage advantages to the employer. The present study, in no sense, embodied a test of any of the recommendations enumerated above but some indications of the magnitudes of likely impact can be gleaned from a closer look at present union policies governing the standard rate and departures from it.

The traditional union attitude toward departures from the standard rate has, of course, been strongly negative, but it is noteworthy that a number of contract clauses allow for wage adjustments to accommodate older workers. The Bureau of Labor Statistics, in a recent analysis of 2,425 collective bargaining agreements, found 247 "specific protection provisions applying to older workers," of which 113 were classified as "pay and hours adjustments."[47]

The degree to which these contract clauses were put to actual use was not explained in the study. But Abrams' questionnaire responses indicated that very little use of the clauses is customarily made. He reported that all of the 31 international reporting, with the exception of the International Typographical Union, refused to permit a superannuated worker to remain at his old job at a lower wage rate.[48] The unions felt that such a policy would weaken the general wage structure, enable employers to take advantage of employees, and set up different wage scales for the same position.

In the present study, five of the twelve Bay area unions were parties to agreements which called for wage adjustments for

[47] *Employment and Economic Status of Older Men and Women,* U. S. Bureau of Labor Statistics, bulletin 1092 (Washington: May, 1952), p. 53.
[48] Abrams, "Unions and the Older Worker," p. 124.

superannuated workers. In general form the contract provisions were almost identical. Each specified "aged" or "handicapped" or "superannuated" workers as subject to special wage adjustment and provided for joint union-employer determination of the appropriate rate, the necessity for mutual agreement conferring effective veto power on each party.

It appears however that the clauses are only rarely used. In both San Francisco and Oakland, the typographical locals negotiated superannuation clauses permitting a rate of pay not less than two-thirds of the journeyman's rate. But in San Francisco there was only one instance of utilization of the provision in the year preceding the interview with the local's president and in Oakland, only a handful of printers had availed themselves of the provision in the last several years.

In fruit and vegetable canning, the secretary of the local union covering the entire Bay area could recall no time at which the provision had actually been employed and another high official in the union declared that the clause had not been used twice in fourteen years.

In fish canning, a similar clause of long standing was described as rarely employed. "The employers seldom bring it up," a union official said. In warehousing, a clause dating back to 1938 had been used perhaps twice since that time according to union officials, and was for all practical purposes inoperative.

The only spark of life sighted in connection with the superannuation clauses was in building service, where several locals were in the process of eliminating the clause from agreements in which it had been written for a number of years. This was, a union representative explained, a response to certain relatively minor annoyances occasioned by the presence of the clauses. Some of the employers, failing to secure union approval for application of the clause, discharged the affected individuals, telling them that the union was at fault. Union officers who had refused the application on the ground that these individuals were entitled to the full wage found themselves confronted by angry members who asserted that the union was not protecting their interests. Union officers, wishing to avoid repetitions, decided to eliminate the clause.

Other locals were simply ignoring the clauses. This was graphically illustrated by a contract held by Local 44 (window cleaners) which specified a $6 per day minimum rate for workers employed under the superannuation provision. This first appeared in 1943 when the daily rate was $9.20. The superannuation minimum remained at $6, though the regular rate had more than doubled since 1943. The provision was simply ignored by the negotiators who did not even bother to bring it up to date.

The principal objections voiced by union officials to extensive use of wage adjustment to accommodate older workers were given as follows:

1. For an initial period, the affected individuals are usually happy at their retention in employment at the reduced rate. Soon, however, they convince themselves that they are doing a full day's work and become dissatisfied at not receiving the full wage.

2. Employers attempt to use the clauses as a lever for general reduction in wages. As it is very difficult to draw the line between the able and the partially able, use of the clause invites difficulties with employers who are not in agreement with the fundamental union position that the provision should be used only in the most extreme situations.

3. The nature of the work in certain labor markets is such that if the worker can do the job at all, he can do it adequately.

4. There are other methods of accommodating older workers who are having difficulty in maintaining the pace.

The nature of some of these objections raises doubts about the extent to which union resistance to departures from the standard rate—and the presence of superannuation clauses in contracts apparently does not reflect a reversal of this policy—should be regarded as adverse to the employment opportunities of older workers.

For example, it seems very doubtful that the failure of the typographical union to make extensive use of the superannuation clauses results in the exit of older printers who would otherwise have found a place in the industry. In fact, the typographical union has erected such a battery of protective practices that wage adjustment as an accommodation for older printers is scarcely necessary. The aged printer is likely to have an ironclad priority (seniority) status; he has the option of part-time work as a result of the "substitute" system; he may be transferred to relatively light work; as a final resort he may accept his pension, and while receiving it, work two days a week. The key, here, obviously lies in the very strong controls imposed throughout the labor market by the typographical union, but a number of the adjustments just cited would be sufficient to retain many older workers in the industry even if employers were freer to make decisions governing hiring and firing than they now are.

Although a number of accommodations can be cited which tend to balance the effects of the standard rate policy on the employment opportunity of older workers already under the protection of the union, the impact of this policy on employer hiring of additional older workers is quite another matter. It seems reasonable to conclude that it must be adverse, yet the important question is the magnitude of the effect. Perhaps some of the considerations listed above operate to discourage the hiring of older workers even where there are no unions to deter employers from wage discrimination.

Special Accommodations

The principal qualifications of the proposition that the union policy of the standard rate has an unfavorable impact on the employment of older workers lie in the existence of alternative procedures for retaining older workers in employment. Shifts to lighter work, whether involving wage reduction or not, appear to be the most prevalent response to the problems arising from the falling efficiency of older workers. Some of these adjustments have been described already in the section dealing with union controls over hiring. Analogous practices exist in those labor markets where the union controls do not extend to this sphere.

A most difficult task in analyzing the mechanisms for accommodation in the various labor markets is to distinguish between the employer and union policies in the prevailing practices. Frequently, it appears, employers pursue generous policies in this respect, while on the other hand, some unions are considerably less militant on behalf of the older workers than others. The mere existence of a contract provision devoted to the procedure for accommodating older workers does not give much information:

it could be the result of a mere codification of a previous employer policy, or it could be evidence of what was mainly union pressure.

On the other hand, the absence of such contract provisions is not very revealing, either. Informal practice may yield as much accommodation as would be found in the presence of some contract provision.

The automobile workers in the Bay area hold a contract with the Kaiser Manufacturing Corporation, Oakland Aircraft Division, which reads in part, "Employees who by reason of advanced age or physical disability are unable to handle their regularly assigned jobs to a reasonable advantage shall be given preference on any available light work." The Ford contract reads in part, ". . . An employee physically incapable of meeting production standards will be given the opportunity to transfer to an operation he is physically capable of performing. . . ." A local official reports that the practices spelled out in the Kaiser and Ford contracts are informally observed at General Motors; however, that company will not agree to the inclusion of such a provision in its collective bargaining agreement.

On the whole, it was not possible to gauge with any accuracy the extent of the disagreement on the issue of special accommodations which exists between union and employer in many of the labor markets investigated, although a number of grievance cases could be cited. Unions have not generally taken the position that older workers should be retained in their old jobs regardless of their declining power, and ordinarily they have not insisted that the higher rates of pay which the older worker had been earning be paid to him if his debility requires a transfer to lower paying work. The argument was only very rarely heard that it is the employer's responsibility to absorb the costs arising from the failing powers of his long-service employees. It seems, therefore, that within a rather broad range there has been substantial agreement between employers and the unions in a number of labor markets. But when disputes have occurred at the margin of this area of agreement, invariably it has been the union which has upheld the position of the older worker. The real differences on the issue have most frequently expressed themselves elsewhere, for example in disputes over whether retirement should be compulsory or voluntary. And as was suggested earlier, employer opposition to the maintenance of older workers can be translated into a generally tougher attitude at the bargaining table in its other dealings with the union.

An important effect of unionism in the sphere presently under discussion is the limitation which is placed on simple discharge of the slowed-up older worker. Most contracts require that employers show cause for discharge, and it is probable that the amount of preparation and litigation which may become necessary in the course of a successful discharge has stayed the hand of the employer in many borderline situations. Again, it is difficult to estimate the relative importance of this consideration. Union officials almost always refer to it as important.

## OTHER POLICIES

### Physical Examinations

Attitudes expressed by union officials about physical examinations were mixed. In general, there was considerably more sentiment which was neutral and definitely favorable toward the practice than seems to be reflected in the standard literature on the subject. This could be the result of the inadequacy of the present sample, or it might arise from the fact that the threat to union security which is implicit in an additional area for discrimination has been considerably attenuated.

The strongest opposition to the practice was voiced by both locals of the electrical workers. Each local has succeeded in prohibiting the practice. Both fought the attempts of shipbuilding companies to institute the practice when many of the electricians were involved in that industry during World War II. Both unions won their fight. The business agent of one local opposed it because it stood as an infringement upon the local's control over the hiring process. The business agent of the other local said it was opposed "on principle."

In the oil refining industry, the unions have not contested the practice which they see as beneficial, but they have taken the position that the findings of the worker's own doctor should take precedence over those of the employer's doctor.

[ 40 ]

Officials of the machinists' union also expressed a favorable attitude toward physical examinations and one of the provisions in the master agreement with the employers' association in the Bay region reads, "The Employer may require employees to take a physical examination." The union feels that the grievance and arbitration machinery, which applies to discharges based on the report of the medical examination, offers sufficient protection against abuse of the practices.

A similar position has been adopted by the sailors, the steelworkers, and the autoworkers. An official of the latter's union recalled what he described as a relatively recent attempt by one company in this area to employ the medical examination too vigorously. Union protests were successfully entered.

On the whole, medical examinations seemed to be a very prevalent practice, at least in the larger firms, and where safeguards in the form of some effective control were present, most unions were not inclined to oppose them.

### Work Load

If one of the important characteristics of the problem facing older workers is the declining ability to perform their work satisfactorily, then policies which are designed to reduce the pace or weight of work for all employees have a disproportionately beneficial effect on the older worker. The effect is to restore him to a position of greater equality with other workers and of more value in the employer's eyes.

Three unions in the present survey have instituted some kind of control over work loads or pace of work in their collective bargaining agreements. An absolute reduction in the pace of work has been brought about in the longshore industry, with the abolition of star gangs and the imposition of load limits and union control, in general.

The contract between Oakland newspapers and the local typographical union specifies a "minimum average" output for linotype operators, performance of which qualifies the operator as "competent to hold a regular situation or to work as a substitute." As Slichter has observed, such "deadlines" confer protection on the slower men.

[ 41 ]

The contract held by the Fish Cannery Workers includes a section under the heading of "Speed-Up." It reads:

The present speed of work for individuals or groups of individuals shall not be increased during the term of this Agreement; provided, however, it is recognized that a fair day's work is expected of all employees.

Officials of other unions varied in their assessment of the importance of the union's impact on the pace of work and of the significance of this impact. In a number of industries, the problem does not seem to have been a serious one. Yet in others, the control of the pace of work was cited as one of the most important achievements of unionism.

The latter attitude was expressed with considerable vigor by officials in the automobile industry, who declared that the danger of "speed up" was, from the union's point of view, an all-pervading, ever-present consideration, and that a large part of the attention of lower union officials was devoted to policing the pace of work.

Steelworker officials also regarded union vigilance over the work load as a major contribution. The wide prevalence of incentive pay systems in that industry causes the problem to express itself in somewhat different forms than are found in the automobile industry, however. In oil refining, an official declared that the work was not exceptionally heavy, but that company officials tend, in the absence of union protest, to make one man responsible for too many operations.

SUMMARY

Available data do not permit good estimates of the magnitude of the impact of union policy on the employment opportunity of the older worker. The study indicated, however, that when the question is put in the following form, "Does the older worker who is a union member fare better with respect to employment opportunity than he would fare in that labor market in the absence of the union?" an affirmative answer is warranted. The relevant policies, in almost every case, have results which are distinctly favorable to the older workers. But at least one policy probably contributes an adverse impact. This is the policy of discouraging or prohibiting downward wage adjustment for those with declining

[ 42 ]

abilities. Yet, is the alternative to permitting such adjustments restricted to the discharge of the older workers in question? Apparently not; frequently they are moved to lower paying jobs, given lighter work, or informally "carried" by other workers. Or the older workers are left in their old jobs at the higher wage rate.

The other policies seem to confer a substantial degree of protection on the older workers. Union controls over hiring limit the power of the employer to discriminate against the older worker on the basis of his age alone. The control over entry is a clear protection against competition of workers outside the protected labor market, and that competition is the basic element in the older worker's insecurity. Union vigilance over physical examinations serves to eliminate unwarranted discriminations in this sphere. The supervision of the pace of work, where the effect has been to reduce it as in longshoring and, most probably, in automobiles and other manufacturing industries, introduces an equalizing feature which is a source of advantage to the older worker. And of course the older worker is clearly the most prominent beneficiary of seniority systems covering layoffs and rehiring. It is very doubtful that the unfavorable impact of the wage adjustment policies counter-balances the favorable effects of the other policies just listed, and it seems reasonable to conclude that unionism makes a positive contribution to the employment opportunity of the older union member.

Whether or not unionism has benefited older workers as a whole is a different question altogether. A number of the policies which confer advantages upon the older union member, constitute burdens on the older worker who is not a union member in a protected labor market. This is especially true where apprentice programs act as the major ports of entry. In the other markets where unions have established the highly protective policies toward the older union worker who is already in the market, as exemplified by the resistance to discharge for falling competence and resistance to wage reduction concessions, employers may react with increased determination to confine their hiring of new employees to younger workers. And where they have done it, it is rare indeed to find evidence of serious union opposition to the employer's discriminatory hiring practices.

[ 43 ]

The complex of union practices which have the most immediate bearing on the older worker's employment opportunity reflects a considerable variety of pressures and motives. To a large degree, the benefits conferred on the older worker spring as by-products from union policies aimed primarily at other ends, the two most important of which are the prosperity of the union membership as a whole and the fundamental security of the union organization. Thus, controls over entry, hiring and layoffs, and vigilance in other areas where discrimination against union members *qua* union members would be possible, have been instrumental in shifting the burden of proof of incapacity onto the employer. This has been accomplished primarily through the institution of relatively unambiguous standards of selection, with the result that discriminations on the basis of age alone have been made more difficult.

In addition to the protection emerging from these basic controls, the older worker is the beneficiary of a number of other policies consciously designed to improve his employment opportunity. The decisions governing the formation of these policies differ materially in character from those just described, for in general the extension of supplementary protection to the older worker involves a cost which must be borne by the rest of the union membership. It may take the form of increased pressures on the union from the employer who for one reason or another prefers fewer older workers. Where the employment of numerous older workers is associated with a substantial decline in efficiency, the costs to the union as a whole may be in terms of the wage rate (as in the case of the electrical workers) or the costs may be in terms of employer ill will which could express itself more generally in a number of other spheres as well. The costs of the subsidy to the older worker may be even more direct if the protection involves the informal carrying of the older worker or the reservation to him of the easier or lighter jobs. Where team incentive operations are in effect, a conflict of interests may become painfully evident. A highly generous policy toward the older worker thus implies that substantial internal as well as external resistances are likely to have been overcome.

On the whole, the supplementary policies did not seem to

[ 44 ]

play a major role in the labor markets investigated. The contract provision requiring that one in five electricians employed be over 55 years of age appeared to be of marginal significance in the two cases observed. The "exempt" category in the case of longshoring amounted to about one per cent of the work force, whereas the jobs set aside for older seamen accounted for only one tenth of one per cent of the total. Of course, it is difficult to assess the significance of such specific policies where the primary "by-product" protections vary so considerably from market to market. By the same token, it is virtually impossible to construct a satisfactory index of union generosity or solicitude for older union members.

Among the unions covered in the present investigation, the scope of the supplementary policies protecting older workers (in the union) was in general the greater where the basic controls secured by the union in the labor market were the stronger and more extensive. Thus, not only did older workers appear to fare better where the union was the stronger because the "by-product" protections were greater, but they also were the beneficiaries of more elaborate supplementary policies designed specifically to enhance their employment opportunity.

Given the strength of the union relative to the employer, the extent of supplementary policies beneficial to the older worker was subject to considerable variation from union to union. Variations in the attitudes of union leaderships seemed to have an appreciable effect on differences in union policies in this sphere. Some union officers appeared to regard protection of the older workers as a matter of "union principle," and a number reported their own efforts to communicate this attitude to other members of the union. One local official periodically schedules membership meetings at which the "old timers" are awarded pins commemorating their long membership—30 years, 40 years, etc.—and at which time the older members are called upon to say few words. When the "old timers" recall the early days of unionism and talk about the times when it was necessary "to wear your union card in your shoe," they gain respect and ultimately some support from the rest of the membership, the official reported. Other officials told of reprimanding younger workers for complaining about the presence of older workers and the need to sacrifice for them. On the other hand, there were some officials who seemed less inclined in this direction and spoke of the propriety of "getting the older fellows out and giving the younger ones a chance." It was clear that concrete differences in attitude prevailed. And, among those unions which control a dispatching service, such differences may be of appreciable importance. On the whole, it seemed that union officials (because they themselves are relatively aged?) expressed a net bias favorable to older workers.

Worsening conditions in the relevant product markets or changing technological conditions bearing adversely on employment exert pressures all along the line of decision governing the degree of protection which the union will confer on the older worker. Such phenomena either weaken the union's bargaining power relative to the employer or raise the price for a given degree of protection to the older worker. In those labor markets where hiring halls distribute work among all the membership, reduced employment is spread more or less evenly over the entire group and the reduced wage income may inspire less feeling for shielding the older worker than exists under higher levels of employment and income. Where reduced employment requires layoffs, the conflict may become acute. A lament by younger workers in one mass-production industry was reported as follows: "We carry the old guys year-in year-out, and now when they could really do something for us, they let us down. Why don't they take the pension and get out?"

A context of unemployment makes it more difficult for union leaders to indulge their personal biases; unemployment always brings internal differences into stronger relief and it may lead to serious factionalism. Officers must give primary attention to the preservation of their own positions and the preservation of the union organization. In such a context, the presence of a pension plan may be a welcome "out" because it drains off some of the pressure set up by unemployment within the union. What appears to be a strong predilection on the part of union officers for liberal pension programs will be discussed in some detail in the next part.

# PART II

## PENSIONS AND RETIREMENT

### PENSIONS

The growth in the number of collectively bargained pension plans has been one of the outstanding "labor" phenomena of the last decade; by mid-1954, coverage of these plans had been extended to over seven million workers.[40] Administration of the pension (and health and other welfare) programs has occasioned important Congressional investigations, and the large and growing accumulations of funds in the welfare programs have come to represent a source of economic power raising a number of questions almost entirely new to collective bargaining and labor organization. A union has used welfare fund monies to purchase a block of stock in a corporation which it was attempting to unionize. At least two others have financed cooperative housing projects for their memberships. And officials in the state of New York have been reported seeking ways to encourage the investment of such funds in large-scale housing developments, because they are "convinced that the billions of dollars in health and pension reserves represent the most fruitful source of new capital for housing construction."[50] The pension programs thus have economic implications extending well beyond the simple welfare function which is performed for older workers who have reached the ends of their working lives. And as noted earlier, the entire "retirement" ques-

[40] *Interim Report of the Subcommittee on Welfare and Pension Funds to the Senate Committee on Labor and Public Welfare* (Washington: 1955), p. 5.
[50] *New York Times*, February 27, 1955.

[ 47 ]

tion has political and social as well as economic implications of a serious and far-reaching nature.

The great proliferation of collectively bargained pension plans since the end of World War II raises two important questions to which the present study bears some relevance. The first has to do with the major purposes served by the pension systems or the major functions performed by them. Why have they been sought so aggressively? How is it possible to explain why pensions have merited such relatively large shares of the "packages" won in recent negotiations? The question, in sum, has to do with the motivations behind the pension demand; it is on this question that the findings of the present study mainly bear.

The second question has to do with the timing of the large-scale appearance of the new industrial pensions. Is there an explanation of their appearance in the post-war and current period? Would it have been more reasonable to have expected the demand to have occurred in the pre-war period or, possibly, to have been deferred to a later era than the one in which it has occurred? Is the present context particularly conducive to growth of the retirement programs? Our study bears only tangentially on this broad question.

In terms of motivation, the statements of the representatives of the unions themselves are inclined to stress the humanitarian aspects of the pension programs which have emerged in the post-war period. The president of the rubber workers union had the following to say late in 1949.[51]

When we are confronted with problems like that of the welfare of our older people we are compelled to seek some adequate solution. . . . When we saw an increasing number of our members being retired on pitifully inadequate incomes, we realized that here was a problem demanding our attention. We saw that in many cases they had to appeal to charities for assistance. We saw other older workers being forced to stay on the payrolls far beyond 65 in order to assure themselves of an income. Certainly the present stage of our technological knowledge does not require that every man work till the day he dies. . . . The present social security setup is like a teaspoon in a bucket when present living costs and the needs of people are considered.

---

[51] L. S. Buckmaster, "Social and Economic Implications of the Pension Drive," address before the 308th meeting of the National Industrial Conference Board (New York: November 22, 1949).

Representatives of the automobile workers union were, during this period, characterizing their own drive for industrial pensions as an effort to secure a "modest standard of living that is consistent with our present day concept of decency and adequacy" for the older worker.[52] Walter Reuther, UAW president, in testifying before the Senate Finance Committee, repeatedly stressed the inadequacy of old age pensions for the support of retired persons. In this connection, the union's own drive for pensions in the automobile industry was characterized as a device to win employer support for expanded Federal social security benefits. Reuther referred to an "overnight" change in the attitude of business leaders toward Federal old age benefits, which he perceived to be in response to union demands for non-contributory private plans in specific industries, notably the automobile industry.[53]

Not all of the pronouncements favoring more adequate assistance to older persons came from the newer unions. During the same period, the late William Green, speaking for the American Federation of Labor, some of whose affiliated unions have for many years financed their own pension programs, called for a broadening of the Social Security system so that a more "realistic" program of support to the elderly could be achieved.[54]

These statements by union representatives expressing concern for the welfare and standard of living of the nation's elderly could be multiplied through even the most casual perusal of convention proceedings, union publications and public statements during the early post-war period. They constitute evidence of at least one major motivation behind the trade union drive for increased retirement benefits. But they do not provide an answer to the second question posed earlier, with respect to the timing of the successful

---

[52] Harry Becker, "Labor's Approach to the Retirement Problem" in *Proceedings,* Industrial Relations Research Association (1950), p. 117. See also Harry Becker, "Labor's Stake in Employment and Retirement," address at the Institute on Living in the Later Years (Ann Arbor, Michgan: August 21, 1949); and Willard E. Solenberger, "Retirement—A Labor Viewpoint," address before the Second International Gerontological Congress (Detroit: September 12, 1951).

[53] *Social Security Revision,* Hearings on H. R. 6000, Testimony of Walter Reuther, Senate Finance Committee, 81st Cong. 2d sess., pt. 3 (Washington: March 15, 1950), pp. 1837–1925.

[54] William Green, "Labor and Our Older Workers," in *Never Too Old* (Albany, New York: New York State Joint Legislative Committee on Problems of the Aging, 1949), p. 101.

drive for pensions. Have not union leaders always stressed the need to care for the aged? Why, then, at this point in time should the burst of pension programs have occurred?

Answers have been offered by a number of observers, but perhaps the most comprehensive has been put forward by Clark Kerr, who has cited five important factors in explanation of the phenomenon.[55] The first is the fact of the changing age distribution of the population as a whole. "The drive for security is one consequence of an aging society. . . ." A second explanation is found in our continuing industrialization with its attendant urbanization, alterations in family life and susceptibility to fluctuations in employment. "Economic progress brought insecurity and insecurity a hunger for security." A third explanation is based on our growing economic welfare. Security is seen as a luxury which can now be afforded by a society which has managed to satisfy the more immediate necessities of life. "Thus it may be that, as the result of enriching our society, the most elemental demands for material goods and services and for leisure have been increasingly satisfied and the need for security seems more important." Similar phenomena have been cited by other writers.

Arthur M. Ross, for example, has suggested that union demands for retirement benefits have perhaps had to wait upon the extension of these benefits generally to the more prosperous elements in the nation's work force.[56]

A characteristic trade union device is to secure for hourly workers those benefits, such as vacation and holiday pay, already enjoyed by the salaried group. Retirement benefits were no exception to the rule.

And a related explanation, one also framed with the primary focus on the beneficial aspects of the pension plans for elderly workers, has been offered by John W. Whittlesey, who saw the demands for pensions as springing from the entrance of labor unions into the "second stage," of a long-run three-stage program, the first aiming at job protection, the second one aiming at "security supplements"

---

[55] Clark Kerr, "The Pension Drive: Social and Economic Implications," address before the 308th meeting of the National Industrial Conference Board (New York: November 22, 1949).

[56] Arthur M. Ross, "The New Industrial Pensions," *Review of Economics and Statistics*, XXXII (May, 1950), 134.

and the third, to come at some time in the future, aiming at "job stabilization," i.e., participation of the union in counter-cyclical policy in general.[57] Pensions, therefore, represented a security supplement to economic welfare which unions, now having passed the first stage, are able to afford for their older members.

A fourth factor offered by Kerr in explanation of the appearance of collectively bargained pension plans in such profusion after World War II is based on the compulsion felt by union leaders to equal or better the benefits won elsewhere in industry. The first dramatic incident in the formation of a pension "pattern" was the Krug-Lewis agreement of 1946 which resulted in pensions for coal miners. This was followed in 1948 by the National Labor Relations Board ruling in the Inland Steel case which declared that pensions were a fit subject for collective bargaining. In the next year, the first major pensions in the steel and automobile industries appeared, and these presumably tipped the balance, converting a tendency into a "pattern" commanding imitation. Exactly how "coercive" is the existence of a pattern of this type? Were the "orbits of coercive comparison," to use Ross' term, primarily facilitating devices for the expression of more basic forces or did they possess intrinsic power of the magnitude required to institute a whole system of retirement benefits? Unfortunately there is no satisfactory way to measure the importance of this force relative to that of the others which were and which may still be operating. It should be noted, in any case, that in citing this force, attention has been diverted from the purely beneficial aspects of pension plans (i.e., from the viewpoint of the older worker) to an institutional or organizational need which the presence of a pension plan helps to satisfy.

This need is the basis for Kerr's fifth explanation of the postwar appearance of the pension drive, the allegiance-provoking function of the plans.[58] The argument is offered that unions have grown so greatly in strength that they now feel able to leave behind the suspicious attitudes toward company-financed plans for-

---

[57] John Whittlesey, "What are Organized Labor's Pension Program Demands?" address before the Distribution Roundtable Luncheon, Washington, D. C. (February 15, 1950).

[58] "Pension plans tie the members more strongly to the union both through gratitude and disciplinary influence. . . ." See Kerr, "The Pension Drive. . . ."

merly held by Samuel Gompers and others. They see pensions as a solidifying device. The experiences of a number of unions to be reviewed below would lend support to this view.

The last two points cited in explanation of the timing of the appearance of the plans bear importantly on the question of motives or the purposes served by pension plans. In his treatment of the new industrial pensions, Ross has also emphasized this beneficial effect of pension systems on organizational solidarity.[50]

To the unions, industrial pensions are a prime source of the institutional security which is still their chief aim in life. Benefits delivered directly to the rank and file through collective bargaining always reflect more credit on the union than those resulting from an act of Congress. Joint administration of pension benefits gives the organization an additional function, a new role, in economic life.

If the general proposition is a good one, one might expect to find a primary source of sentiment favorable to pension programs in the union's top leadership, for it is the incumbent leadership which is most acutely aware of "union security" or "institutional security" of the type referred to above; it is the leadership which feels the first effects of alterations in this sphere. Yet it is most difficult to secure good evidence of this phenomenon. All demands are served on the employer by union leadership. It is difficult enough for the outsider to discover which demands are being pressed in negotiations and which are being brought forward merely as window dressing; it is almost impossible to distinguish between those being pushed especially hard by the leadership for the benefit of the leadership and those pushed by the leadership for the benefit of the membership. In the case of pensions, for example, how could the two benefits be separated out?

It would be easier to identify the position of the leadership *qua* leadership on the issue of pensions if the internal divisions on this issue were of a more serious nature. But the sentiment favoring pensions seems to be shared by the old and the leadership and the young. This is not to imply that there have not been differences between old and young. In fact, there have been some. But they have been of a considerably milder and less pervasive nature than observers of some instances of conflict early in the

---

[50] Ross, *op. cit.*, p. 136.

pension drive seemed to fear they would be.[60] The conclusion suggested by the experience in a number of unions reviewed below, and especially the longshore union, is that although younger workers may prefer current wage increases more strongly than the older workers, they are able to recognize tangible benefits to themselves in pension plans whose effect is to induce the older worker to leave the labor market and, thus, reduce the competition for easier work or more work or more highly paid jobs.

But the significant point is that incumbent leadership has been very active in pointing out these benefits to the younger members. This has been the case in several situations investigated in the present study. The fact is that incumbent leadership does seem to have thrown its weight behind the pension demands. Where there has been open conflict on the issue among the industries investigated—the most spectacular occurred in the automobile industry when the pension issue first arose—incumbent leadership has favored and insurgent leadership opposed instituting or increasing pension benefits. Where conflict has been below the surface or in lesser degree, the position of incumbent leadership is considerably more difficult to isolate. Yet, in the course of the numerous interviews undertaken in the present study, some hazy outlines of leadership policy seemed to emerge. The typical official admitted the presence of a "few" dissident younger members in connection with the extension of benefits to older workers. These "few" were regarded as lacking in "union principles," where the latter term is defined to include a decent respect for the welfare of older members.[61] The standard treatment, as reported, has been to exhort the dissidents in terms of "union principles." Sometimes these exhortations include references to the fact that the older

---

[60] "Given the fact that younger persons cannot be expected to be as interested in pensions as are those nearer retirement age, pensions seem likely to increase the already existing schism in unions between older and younger men. Such a cleavage can be a significant factor in union demands and in internal union politics." Herbert R. Northrup, "Collective Bargaining on Pensions," in Anne P. Cook, editor, *Pensions and Health and Welfare Plans in Collective Bargaining* (Berkeley: Institute of Industrial Relations and University Extension, University of California, April 13, 15, 1950), p. 14. See also the comments by Dunlop, Slichter and Stigler noted above.

[61] In reporting these responses, the author has already applied what he regards as an appropriate discount for the desire of union officials to display humanitarian impulses.

men "built the union." Sometimes the younger men are asked to look to the future when they themselves will be approaching old age. Sometimes the advantages of eliminating the older men are recited and in this connection numerous officials have stated the belief that at some point the older men should get out and "give the younger men a chance." It is noteworthy, however, that this latter point of view was never expressed without reference to adequate retirement benefits as the device to facilitate the exit.

The kind of evidence just cited is of a highly tenuous sort and might be hardly worth reporting were there not other similar wisps of evidence with which to group it. And one of these has to do with the alacrity with which union officers seem to turn to pension programs as a means to reduce unemployment or under-employment in their respective labor markets. Their concern over the problem and the solutions they consider often precede the response of the "rank-and-file," and sometimes precede the appearance of the phenomenon of unemployment itself. The mere anticipation of an unemployment situation seems in some instances to have disposed leadership favorably toward the institution of pension plans or the improvement in benefits in existing plans. This has certainly been true in the telephone industry and leaders in the oil refining union have also demonstrated a remarkable sensitivity to unemployment.[62] Altogether, incumbent leadership appears to lead rather than to lag behind in the matter of instituting or improving pension benefits.

The proposition that pension programs are at least in part a response to unemployment fits well with the notions put forward by Kerr and Ross respecting "institutional security" as a primary motive behind the pension demand. The internal implications of unemployment have not been fully analyzed in the literature of union politics, but it is apparent that leadership is more comfortably situated in the absence of unemployment than in its presence. Unemployed members mean dissatisfied members and often factionalism. Frequently, in such contexts, internal conflict is carried on to the tune of increased pressure from the employers. It is easy to see why leadership may be especially sensitive to the approach of a situation of unemployment. It is, after all, especially vulner-

---

[62] See pp. 64–66 below.

able to it. But the general proposition linking unemployment and pension benefit programs, does not of course, rest solely on the position taken by union leadership. It is based fundamentally, on the community of interest of all important elements within the union, the old and the young as well as the leadership.

How generally are pension programs regarded by unions as devices to clear the market of an excess supply of labor? Were the two instances to be described later, in which the presence of especially high rates of unemployment served to evoke union support of compulsory retirement, unique? Such support has been a relatively rare policy among unions. Yet it would seem from an examination of some of the other unions included in the present survey that these positions, though extreme did not betray a fundamentally unique view of the function of pension plans. A number of other unions clearly regarded the industrial pensions as devices to eliminate the elderly workers as well as devices to confer leisure and security upon them. And it would seem that in periods of rising unemployment the former function climbs rapidly in relative importance.

There has been some mention of this aspect of the union pension programs in the recent literature.[63] But on the whole it has been given less emphasis than it appears to merit. The institution of the mine workers' pension, the first great industrial plan in the post-war period, occurred, after all, in an industry which had experienced rapid technological change and declining demand for its product. As a result the industry suffered from chronic underemployment. The next two great pension systems to come into being occurred in the steel and automobile industries during a slump which union leaders feared might develop into the long-awaited "post-war depression." On the surface, at least, it would appear that the hypothesis linking employment pressures and pension programs is a promising one. In the present study, the experience of a number of the unions gave it additional support.

The post-war plight of the West Coast longshore union has been briefly described in Part I. There were too many men on the docks for the work which was available. Rotary dispatch,

---

[63] See Industrial Relations Counselors, Inc., "Age and Other Requirements for Retirement on Pension," *Industrial Relations Memos*, No. 129 (May 15, 1953).

which distributes employment evenly, left everyone underemployed. Dissatisfaction from this source combined with older conflicts to provoke serious internal strife, one effect of which was the loss by incumbent leadership of control over the key San Francisco local. It was the arrival of the Korean War which finally relieved the union of the severe pressures emanating from unemployment.

And well before the end of the Korean War, the union had negotiated a pension plan (with a compulsory retirement feature) the effect of which already has been a substantial decline in the registration in those ports most affected by the earlier unemployment conditions.

The pension plan which became effective in July 1952 was negotiated in the preceding year. It is financed wholly through employer contributions and, compared to most of the collectively bargained plans in major industries in existence at that time—and for that matter, those existing now—it is an extremely generous one. The pension amounts to $100 per month exclusive of social security benefits, after 25 years of service.

It is, of course, not possible to gauge with any accuracy the relative importance of the major purposes motivating the union leadership in the negotiation of this plan. As it has turned out, the pension plan has been very popular and, according to reports from both union and management spokesmen, it has operated as an important solidifying force. That the plan was valued by the leadership simply for the welfare which it dispensed to older longshoremen can, no doubt, be taken for granted. And it is probably true that the existence of newly-won pensions in other industries stood as a challenge to the longshore union to do as well or better for its membership. Yet however important these considerations stood in the thinking of the leadership it seems very probable that both the prospect of unemployment with the return of more normal times and the problem of general productivity (as discussed earlier) served as strong stimulants for the institution of this program, the effect of which was calculated to retire 3,769 longshoremen—well over one-fifth of the total work force—during the 10-year period of the plan's span.

The age distribution of longshoremen at the time of the first negotiations for the pension plan indicates something of the effect which the wholesale retirements should have on the potentiality, at any rate, for increases in worker efficiency. Table II gives two estimates of age distribution for longshoremen, for 1949, one a union estimate based on a large sample, the other an estimate for the same year made after a survey by actuaries hired by the employers. In addition, comparable data are supplied for the elec-

## TABLE II
### Age Distribution of Selected Union Groups and of All Employed Males in California

| Age Group | Pacific Coast Longshoremen, 1949 | | International Brotherhood of Electrical Workers, February, 1953 | | International Typographical Union, May, 1951 | All Employed Males in California |
|---|---|---|---|---|---|---|
| | Union Estimate | Employer Estimate | San Francisco | Oakland | Entire Membership | |
| | (1) | (2) | (3) | (4) | (5) | (6) |
| Under 35....... | 12.5 | 10.1 | 25.4 | 27.6 | 16.0 | 37.7 |
| 35–44.......... | 27.3 | 27.2 | 28.0 | 26.2 | 27.0 | 25.8 |
| 45–54.......... | 30.5 | 32.2 | 28.3 | 27.8 | 28.5 | 19.8 |
| 55–64.......... | 21.8 | 22.0 | 16.0 | 16.6 | 20.9 | 12.5 |
| 65 and over..... | 7.9 | 8.4 | 2.2 | 1.7 | 7.5 | 4.3 |
| Total...... | 100.0 | 99.9 | 99.9 | 99.9 | 99.9 | 100.1 |

SOURCES: Col. (1)—Research Dept., ILWU.
Col. (2)—Marsh & McLennan, San Francisco, Longshore Pension Study, Draft 3.
Col. (3) and (4)—International Brotherhood of Electrical Workers, Washington, D.C.
Col. (5)—"Annual Reports of Officers," *Typographical Journal*, supplement, CXXI (July, 1952), 54S.
Col. (6)—*United Census of Population: 1950*, Vol. II, Part 5, p. 256.

trical workers (taken from Table I in Part I), for members of the International Typographical Union whose membership has generally been considered among the most aged of the craft unions, and for all employed males in the state of California.

The data in Table II indicate that the longshoremen as a group were more aged even than the typographical union membership. And it is certain, since entry was closed during the period, that in the course of the three years between the date of the age surveys and the effective date of the pension program, the longshore membership aged still more.

The pension proposal made by the union to the waterfront employers association included a provision for automatic retirement at age 68. This provision appears in the plan and stands as evidence of the union's view of the pension plan as a device to bring about the exit of the older workers. One high official has declared that the principal function of the compulsory retirement provision was to serve as a guarantee to the younger members in exchange for their support of the plan, of immediate relief from the large quantity of informal "covering" of older workers and of an immediate opening up of a number of the easier and more highly desired jobs to which the most elderly workers had gravitated. And of course the basic guarantee consisted of assurance of more work per man in a reduced work force in the event of a recurrence of low employment conditions.

It was anticipated that some objections to the compulsory retirement provision would arise and these anticipations have been fulfilled in the case of the older clerks whose work is less arduous than that of the longshoremen. Yet on the whole, union officials greatly underestimated the number of men between the ages of 65 and 68 who have, to date, elected to retire voluntarily. It seems quite possible, in view of this experience and in view of the entirely different "age" context in which the next plan will be negotiated, that the ILWU position on compulsory retirement will undergo change.

One significant aspect of a number of the older as well as some of the more recently instituted pension plans is the proviso that members of the union who accept the pension are prohibited from engaging in further work in their respective labor markets. The pension plan of the International Brotherhood of Electrical Workers contains such a prohibition.[64] As the prohibition does not apply to work in other industries or to income received from other sources, it seems safe to assume that the provision is not aimed at realizing some principle of equity in income distribution, but rather is directed at insuring that the benefit program does indeed reduce the supply of electricians in the contracting field.

[64] "Any member of the Brotherhood who accepts a pension payment for any particular month under the provisions of this Agreement shall thereby cancel any claim he may have against the Pension Benefit Fund of the Brotherhood for the same month, and he agrees not to perform any electrical work of any kind either for compensation or gratis for anyone." Article III, Section 5, Employees Benefit Agreement, National Electrical Benefit Fund of the National Employees Benefit Board for the Electrical Contracting Industry.

This pension is a contributory one, of course, and it may be taken for granted that union members are not indifferent to the uses to which the deductions from their wages are put. As indicated earlier, the union has a stake in the level of worker efficiency which is maintained. Although the business managers of both locals made it clear that the retirement decision was left entirely to the individual electrician, there seemed to be the feeling that the locals had somewhat less of an obligation to find suitable work for the aging and slowed-up electrician if he was eligible for a pension than if he had not yet reached the retirement age.

Two other unions among those covered in the present survey imposed limits on the participation of pension recipients in their respective labor markets.

The typographical union does not prohibit work by pensioners but it limits the amount of work to two days per week during any week in a pension month in which a pension check is drawn.[65] This pension is wholly financed through membership contribution and is the only plan so financed among the unions under investigation in the present study. As the solvency of the pension fund has been a continuing issue before the printers, there seems to be a general reluctance on the part of printers to retire while they are still able to work. It is interesting that the language of the benefit provisions in the Book of Laws tends to discourage retirement rather than to encourage it. Formally, pensions are made available to those eligible in age and years of service only if they are "unable to continue in or secure sustaining employment because of age or disability." Actually, there is no way to refute the individual who reports himself "unable to continue" in employment. It seems reasonable to assume—and the testimony of local officers tends to corroborate it—that both the reluctance of the individual printer

[65] As this limitation applies not only to work in the printing industry but to any work at all, it would appear that the principle of individual need has been incorporated into the regulations. The regulation reads, "Pensioners may engage in a pursuit inside or outside the trade, but shall not be eligible for the pension in any four-week pension period that money received as wages shall exceed the sum equivalent to eight days' pay at the scale of the union with which pensioner is affiliated. . . ." Book of Laws of the International Typographical Union (1952), p. 71. This provision is based on the notion, evidently, that if an ex-printer can make a living in another trade and chooses to do so, there is no need to burden the union with the payment of a pension check. Possibly, the fact that the pension is wholly self-financed accounts for this attitude.

to retire while he still is physically able to work and the generally negative tone toward retirement at the normal retirement age expressed in the Book of Laws is explained at least in part by the fact that the plan is a self-financed one. The individual printer who has for many years witnessed the struggle of his union to keep its pension fund solvent is reluctant to burden the union with his upkeep. And the union itself is acutely aware of the enormous costs entailed in encouraging and financing early retirement among the majority of its eligible members. Some of the considerations involved here have never been faced by most unions, and this may account, in part, for diversity in policy with respect to some aspects of the retirement question. There is evidence, however, that recognition of some of the problems faced for many years by the printers is becoming more general.

The concern over the financial stability of the pension fund expressed in the generally negative attitude of the eligibility rule is subject to considerable alteration in periods of underemployment in the trade. Under these conditions the general disposition is to encourage retirements among those eligible so that the available work can be distributed among the most needy. Within the typographical union during the depression of the thirties, strong informal pressures were exerted by the membership as a whole on the older printers to leave the industry if they could support themselves with the pension and other sources of income. The social pressures, it should be noted, are particularly effective in this union.

The pension program instituted recently by the Sailors Union of the Pacific contains a prohibition against the continued participation of pensioners in the labor market.[66] Does this reflect an inclination to view the pension program as a device to clear the market of excess seamen? One high union official volunteered the information that this was indeed one of the purposes of the plan. And there is other evidence to indicate that its performance along this line is a welcome function from the point of view of the sailors as a group, especially in view of the substantial decline in the

---

[66] "In the pension plan, a man does not have to retire at 65—as is the rule in some unions—if he does not want to—but once he takes his pension he cannot compete for jobs under the jurisdiction of the Sailors Union." *West Coast Sailors,* September 4, 1953.

volume of shipping through West Coast ports since the end of the Korean War and the resulting rise in unemployment among the seamen.

The fact that the pension plan was not instituted until 1954 was especially interesting because there is considerable evidence that the sailors union could have had such a plan earlier but refused it. Instead, the union was content to secure increased employer contributions to a jointly-administered welfare fund which union spokesmen described as a plan "tailored to the needs of the group of men going to sea for a living." The SUP plan, it was pointed out, was "not a copy of someone else's plan as are most."[67] The report of the union trustees, at the end of 1952, noted[68]

The Board, from the beginning, refused to take the easy course of using Welfare Plans of other industries as a pattern. It recognized that sailors and their problems differed widely from workers in other fields, and it was determined to fashion a plan aimed at bringing full benefits to men that sailed for their livelihood. . . .

Readily apparent, the most important immediate needs proved to be aid to the old-timer forced to retire from the sea, and aid to those physically disabled, either permanently or temporarily. . . .

After many surveys and much study, the Board discovered that one of the distinctions of the group of men that go to sea for a living was that many have no families.

This fact, as well as the limited supply of money in the Fund, led the Board to adopt a policy that benefits sailors—*while they are alive and in need.* It will not benefit some third cousin and other relative when an old-timer has passed on after devoting his life to the sea. (Italics in original).

Flexibility seems always to have been the keynote in the administration of the Welfare Fund and the trustees listed a large number of miscellaneous services which had been performed for needy members. For example, "The cost of transporting the body of a sailor to his home in Oklahoma was borne by the Fund. . . . A sailor, ineligible for Marine Hospital service, was fitted out with an artificial leg which makes possible fitness to sail again. . . . A speaking aid was provided for a sailor who lost his voice due to a cancer operation."[69]

---

[67] "Report on Sailors Home of the Pacific (SUP Welfare Fund)," *West Coast Sailors,* January 23, 1953.
[68] *Ibid.*
[69] *Ibid.*

Older sailors received a number of benefits from the Fund. In fact, some were receiving a form of pension. "To date the Fund has paid monthly allowance benefits to 85 oldtimers and to 104 disabled sailors."[70] The primary form of assistance to sailors who had become too old to work, however, was to be a system of subsidies, the most important of which was housing. As the trustees reported[71]

Originally, the Sailors Union membership went on record to build a home in the country to take care of disabled and older sailors. After canvassing the oldtimers up and down the coast, it was found that the overwhelming majority were opposed to leaving their home ports. As a result, this plan was temporarily shelved, or rather broadened.

Sailors' hotels in all coast ports are now being planned. These will serve the dual purpose of providing a home for the retired oldtimer who wishes to live there, and a place where, between ships, or while convalescing from illness, a sailor may live in congenial, clean and decent quarters for a nominal price.

In the early part of December, 1952, a 16-unit "pilot" project was opened in the Port of Wilmington. Immediately, it was "filled to capacity by oldtimers who pay a rental of $15.00 monthly which includes all utilities such as light, heat, water, etc." The rent charge was indeed nominal. The apartments consisted of "a combination living room and bedroom head and galley" and were "fully equipped with frigidaire, stove and furniture." The $15 per month rental was levied in consideration of a state law which would have caused a reduction in state benefits in the absence of the rental charge.

The Fund's trustees announced plans to erect such hotels in all coast ports and by the beginning of 1953, lots close to the union halls in both San Francisco and Wilmington were purchased for the purpose.

Before the year was out, however, the emphasis in the program to care for elderly seamen had been shifted to a pension plan. A survey of the membership had indicated considerable sentiment in favor of such a plan and the union publication announced that as of the first of August some 86 per cent of mem-

[70] *Ibid.*
[71] *Ibid.*

[62]

bers responding to union queries had favored a pension plan.[72] A few weeks later, announcement was made that negotiations with the employers had resulted in agreement on an employer-financed pension program yielding benefits of $100 per month, exclusive of Social Security benefits to sailors (with 20 years of "Qualifying Time") reaching the age of 65. Some time after this, Harry Lundeberg, SUP leader, announced that $800,000 was being transferred from the Welfare Fund to the pension fund.[73]

An explanation of this turn of events might run along the following lines: that sailors, having tried other devices, became gradually convinced that pensions were a superior form of benefit to the aged. But there is no evidence of "failure" of the earlier approach in any important sense. A somewhat more plausible hypothesis is that the presence of a liberal pension program for the neighboring and, in many respects, rival longshoremen—instituted in the middle of 1952—served as a spur to the institution of the sailors' plan. It is clear that the elderly longshoremen were enthusiastic about the program; the sailors and their leaders may well have changed their views as a result of it. And there is also strong evidence that increasing unemployment provided a special stimulus to the institution of the pension plan. By the late summer of 1953, the union's publication reported, "Marine Employment Down 25% from Early '52 Total,"[74] and the union's hiring hall was filling up with unemployed sailors. That the new pension plan was regarded by the union officials as a partial solution to the problem of unemployment can be seen in the official announcement by the negotiating committee which was carried in the organization's publication. "Altogether the Pension plan should not only be a great help to the men who are growing older—but by encouraging them to retire will no doubt help shipping."[75] In another place, the report stated

This Pension Plan will tend to open up more jobs because a man can, now, if he wants to and has the time in, retire any time between

---

[72] These responses were not made available for study and it is not clear exactly what the statistic signifies. Union officials declared, however, that the response was large.

[73] *Ibid.*, January 8, 1954.

[74] *Ibid.*, August 21, 1953.

[75] *Ibid.*, September 4, 1953.

60 and 65 and according to our records there will be approximately 200 men able to qualify by January 1. Of course, as years go on, this number goes up.

By June, 1954, the union reported that some 150 sailors had elected to take the pension and withdraw from the industry.[76] And a union official interviewed in August of the same year, when he was asked if he thought the pension would substantially improve the employment situation, replied: "Yes, about 200 are already on pension. That's what pension plans are for—to drain the older guys off the labor market. We encourage the older guys to get out and give the younger ones a chance."

As the discussion of union policy toward compulsory retirement will reveal, officials in at least one local in the oil refining industry were quick to associate unemployment as a problem with retirement as a partial solution. As a result, there came the request that automatic retirement be instituted in order to relieve the pressure of unemployment. Such a policy, though not unique in union experience, has been relatively rare. In the oil refining industry, particularly, another kind of solution to the problem of unemployment seems to have more general support. This, as has been discussed in some detail in an earlier section, is the institution of a shorter work week. But the great emphasis which has been put on the reinstitution of the 36-hour work week by union leaders should not obscure the fact that, despite some general reluctance to endorse compulsory retirement provisions, the retirement (i.e., pension) route has not been overlooked as a device to clear the market of some of the excess labor.

The oil workers union leadership evidently sees early retirement as the suitable policy to promote in this sphere and at least one top policy group has recommended increased pension benefits to induce the older oil refinery workers to leave the industry. This group was the Coalition Council of the National Coalition of Oil Unions which had been convened to discuss problems common to all unions in the oil industry and to consider the possibility of amalgamation. The official publication of the Oil Workers International Union-CIO, reported the following:[77]

[76] *Ibid.*, June 25, 1954.
[77] *International Oil Worker*, September 21, 1953.

Decreased employment and layoffs in the oil industry was the major subject of discussion at a meeting of the Coalition Council of the National Coalition of Oil Unions held in Chicago, September 13.

As a result of the discussions, the Council recommended that the various unions participating seek these changes in their contracts:

1. Stand-by clauses which would provide for a change to the 36-hour work week if and when the employment situation in the industry warrants such change.

2. Improved pensions to provide for retirement at age 60.

3. Longer vacations.

All of these things would lessen unemployment in the oil industry.

What is rather surprising in this situation is that the remedial measures, including pension plan revision, seem to have been suggested to the union by an employment dip of very small size. According to a bulletin carried in the *International Oil Worker* in the summer of 1954, employment in the industry for the first quarter of the year had declined from the 1953 average by only four per cent.[78]

The major telephone workers union has for many years proposed the institution of an early retirement scheme. Sentiment in favor of this plan can be traced in large measure to many long service employees who themselves desire to leave the industry on pension. But at least on one occasion the early retirement proposal has been put forth as a device to ease unemployment in the industry.

Actually, employment has been very steady in the telephone industry since the end of the war. However, the major unions have always feared the prospect of displacement arising from the important technological developments which occurred continuously in the industry. As it has turned out, the secular increase in the demand for telephone service has, until recently, quite overbalanced the adverse employment effects of technological change. But this has not always been apparent from any point of time looking into the future, and the union leadership has made numerous studies of employment prospects in the industry.

Perhaps the chief concern of the union officials has been over

[78] *Ibid.*, July 26, 1954. It is possible, however, that union leadership was responding to what appears to be a secular decline in the demand for production workers in oil refining. Employment was 147,000 in 1948 and only 137,000 in 1954, though production was up 22 per cent over the period. See *CIO News*, September 27, 1954.

the increasing dial mechanization with its threat to the employment prospects of operators. Until recently only local traffic was being converted from manual to dial operation, but this was sufficient to cause concern. At the end of World War II only somewhat more than half of the Bell System's telephones had been converted to dial for local calling, and the immediate future promised the rapid conversion of the rest of the system to dial. The National Federation of Telephone Workers appointed a committee composed chiefly of representatives of the traffic operators to investigate employment prospects and in view of this technological development, make recommendations for a solution.

This committee estimated that some 65,000 jobs were in jeopardy, and recommended a transitional program which rested very heavily upon a liberal early retirement scheme as a device to drain off the elderly among the currently employed operators. In 1951 a similar group, the Technological Advancement Committee, made an almost identical proposal, calling for an improved pension plan to "... permit voluntary retirement after 25 years of service.... This would help to offset the condition of fewer job openings due to mechanization of the industry...."[70]

It should be mentioned that in at least one union, the machinists, the leadership was far from enthusiastic about inaugurating a vigorous pension program. The policy of the international union with regard to pensions amounts mainly to an educational program aimed at alerting local unions to many of the pitfalls of pension financing and administration; actual bargaining authority resides at the local level. Officials of the union in the Bay area reported that they were not making pension demands. The main reason offered for this position was that the nature of the industry makes it very difficult to institute pension programs. The president of a San Francisco local union representing some 5,000 machinists stated that his organization had members in about 600 different firms. He felt that private pension plans were not feasible in the metal trade for this reason. The business agent of the East bay district organization also emphasized this point. He said that the consensus at district headquarters was that re-

---

[70] *Report of Technological Advancement Committee to the CWA-CIO Executive Board* (February 5, 1951), p. 3.

[ 66 ]

tirement security should be achieved through the expansion of existing government programs.

The position of the unions is somewhat complicated by the fact that a number of the larger firms with whom they hold contracts have already instituted pension programs. Current practice in the Bay area, it was reported, calls for scrutiny of these plans to see that they accord with "our principles." Two points made in elaboration of this statement were opposition to compulsory retirement and opposition to provisions withholding service credit for time lost during strikes.

An impression gained from the discussions with the local, district and international representatives was that IAM policy on the question of pensions had not yet completely jelled. Local unions find themselves in a somewhat uncomfortable position with some of their members covered by pension programs while others are not. The union does not feel that it can afford to ignore the existing plans because the members covered by them have a clear interest in the benefits levels and many other aspects of the plans. But at the same time, forceful demands for higher benefits in existing pension plans would only bring into sharper focus the current inactivity with respect to the institution of new plans. Yet, if the extension of pension benefits to the bulk of the membership is to occur, it will probably have to be done on the union's initiative and through the institution of an "area plan" of the sort introduced by the auto workers. But an area plan entails the assumption of many administrative and financial responsibilities which the unions have not yet been willing to assume. The chief officer in the East bay district reported that very little thought had been given to the idea of adopting such a plan. In any case, no action in this direction had been taken at the time of the survey. Present policy, thus, represents something of an uneasy compromise between action and inaction on the pension issue. Officials interviewed were unanimous in asserting that they did not oppose pensions on principle, but rather because of the impracticability of private pensions in their industry. Nor was the possibility of a change in policy completely ruled out. One international representative, in fact, reported "quite a bit of pension sentiment among the people in Southern California."

The evidence supporting the thesis that unions see pension programs as a device to reduce the pressure of unemployment could be multiplied without settling the larger question which has to do with the magnitude of the effort which unions will exert to secure the larger pensions. And this, after all, is the most important consideration from the point of view of the question raised in the introduction concerning the ultimate "economic burden" which the community will decide to bear in support of its elderly.

Thus, while it is significant that the late vice president of the giant United Steelworkers of America should refer to pensions as "most helpful shock absorbers" in periods of declining economic activity,[80] the more significant datum is the percentage of currently won gains which the steel union is allocating to the pension fund.

It appears that in the mass production industries, the pension share of current "packages" is large, and if the pronouncements of high union officials in such industries as the steel and automobile industries can be taken at face value they are likely to continue to be large for some time to come. The automobile workers have already established a minimum pension well in excess of $200 per month as a bargaining objective, and their most recent bargaining settlements have provided for substantial improvements in pension benefits levels.

There is a possibility, because the plans are new and because most are financed entirely by the employer, that union memberships have not fully realized the extent of the expenditure which is being made for pensions. Allocating 5 cents of a 12-cent "package" to pensions really means spending over $8.00 per month per man for pensions. Would union members have been equally satisfied with a 12-cent per hour increase in the wage rate and a dues increase of $8.00 per month earmarked for pensions? Those unions which have financed their own pension plans through membership contributions (e.g., the printers, and, until recently, the electrical workers) have never failed to bewail the high cost of their plans. An official of the typographical union has declared, for example, that his union's main problem ". . . is not so much in

---

[80] Report of speech by James G. Thimmes in Steel Labor, November 1954.

finding work for our older members as it is to find enough money for them to retire on."[81] And the income of printers is substantially higher *and* more steady than those of most workers, a substantial part of whose bargaining gains have been taken recently in the form of pension programs. Is it possible that the discrepancy implicit in this comparison has been made possible by some special energy on the part of the union leaderships which have negotiated the new plans and the current improvements in them? i.e., have union leaders used some form of "money illusion" for the purpose of strengthening the union's (and their own) security through the pursuit of pensions?

## RETIREMENT PRACTICES

Published material from union sources almost always emphasizes a strong opposition to the principle of compulsory retirement.[82] A survey of 300 collectively bargained pension plans led Rowe and Paine to the conclusion that "Labor organizations are virtually unanimous in their opposition to such compulsory retirement provisions."[83] And the authors conclude on the basis of their study:[84]

Generally, the analysis revealed that the greater the degree of union participation in the administration of the plans the less likely were they to contain compulsory retirement provisions.

Most of the unions covered in the present study evidence some opposition to a fixed retirement age. This statement leaves a lot unsaid, however, because the degree of opposition offered varied considerably. Some indicated that they had been opposed

---

[81] Charles W. Campbell, "Labor Views its Elderly Workers," in *Never Too Old* (Albany, New York: New York State Joint Legislative Committee on Problems of the Aging, 1949), pp. 98–100.

[82] See, for example, Solomon Barkin, "Should There Be a Fixed Retirement Age? Organized Labor Says No," in Clark Tibbitts, editor, *Social Contribution by the Aging* (Philadelphia: American Academy of Political and Social Science, 1952), pp. 77–80; Harry Block, "What Labor Union Practices Promote Employment of Older Workers," in *The Problem of Making a Living While Growing Old* (Temple University and Pennsylvania Department of Labor and Industry, September, 1952), pp. 155 ff; Solenberger, *op. cit.* The official pension handbook of the AFL definitely opposes the compulsory principle in retirement programs.

[83] Evan K. Rowe and Thomas H. Paine, "Pension Plans Under Collective Bargaining Agreements: II—Compulsory Retirement," *Monthly Labor Review*, 76 (May, 1953), 489.

[84] *Ibid.*, p. 485.

at one time in the past and then had let the matter drop. Others fought more stubbornly or had more power to bring to bear and managed to eliminate the provision. However, most did not. Plans subject to collective bargaining contained compulsory retirement features in eight labor markets investigated in the present study while in four, there were no such compulsory provisions.[85]

Union attitudes in the present study were far from unanimous even apart from variations in the vigor with which the official positions were defended. A number of unions were at least indifferent to compulsory retirement and one union (and a local of another) actively sponsored it.[86] An inquiry into the backgrounds of these diverse attitudes constitutes the major business of the present chapter.

Opposition to Compulsory Retirement.

1. *Union Plans*

Two of the unions under study in the present investigation have for many years financed and administered their own pension plans. In neither is retirement mandatory at a fixed age.

The typographical workers pension is wholly financed and administered by the union. There is no age at which retirement is required; in fact, as noted earlier, the rules governing pension eligibility require that the applicant be "unable to continue in or secure sustaining employment because of age or disability,"[87] a provision which on the face of it, at least, would seem to encourage printers to remain in the trade until the highest possible chronological age.

The electrical workers have a pension plan which was formerly wholly financed through membership contributions but which since 1947 has been partly financed through employer contributions. The union has never included a fixed retirement age in its pension program, and local officers interviewed expressed an-

---

[85] In the same way, despite the virtually unanimous union opposition to compulsory retirement noted by Rowe and Paine, 175 of the 300 bargained plans embodied compulsory retirement provisions.

[86] Some diversity in union attitudes on this issue has been noted by Industrial Relations Counselors, *op. cit.* See also Helen Baker, *Retirement Procedures under Compulsory and Flexible Retirement Policies* (Princeton, New Jersey: Princeton University, Industrial Relations Section, 1952).

[87] *Book of Laws of the International Typographical Union* (1952), p. 70.

[ 70 ]

tipathy to the idea, deploring the principle of compulsion as contrary to its philosophy of accommodation and protection of the individual member.

## 2. Bargained Plans

The first expressions of union opposition to automatic retirement were made considerably before the postwar outcropping of pension programs offered the opportunity for regular negotiation of disputed provisions. As a rule, two grounds were offered for the objection to the practice. Unions objected that the retirement was, in effect, a discharge without sufficient cause[88] or they argued that it was a layoff violating the seniority provisions. A number of these disputes ended in arbitration and the rulings of arbitrators have tended to uphold the position of the respective employers, though there have been some exceptions, to be sure.[89] One such decision favorable to the union occurred in the case of the Fish Cannery workers of Monterey. Yet despite this decision and a seven-day strike in which the issue figured prominently, the union was not able to secure elimination of the practice.

In 1947 two employees of a large packing firm with which the union held a contract were released from their jobs because their age exceeded the company's retirement age. The employees complained to the union which carried the case through the grievance procedure and finally to arbitration. The union contended that the retirement amounted to a discharge without sufficient cause and that the contract had been violated. The arbitrator found in favor of the union and ordered reinstatement of the two men with back pay.[90]

---

[88] See Abrams, "Unions and the Older Worker," p. 123, who reports that questionnaire responses indicated unanimous opposition by unions to discharge for age alone.

[89] A number of arbitration awards are cited in Barkin, "Union Policies and the Older Worker," p. 82. An additional ruling not cited is: *In the Matter of Arbitration Between United Packinghouse Workers of America and Swift & Company* (July 5, 1946). Arbitrator Charles O. Gregory found that the company "may, in the exercise of its management prerogatives, retire any employee or terminate his or her employment, because of age, as long as the exercise of this right, in any particular instance, is in conformance to its established policy and is not arbitrary, discriminatory or capricious."

[90] Award of Arbitrator Kalman Y. Sapero in the case of the *AFL Fish Cannery Workers Union of the Pacific, Monterey County on behalf of Fred Knowles and Charles Goger, Complainant vs. California Packing Corporation and Monterey Fish Processors Association, Respondents* (July 29, 1947).

Two days after the award was made, however, the union's contract expired and company negotiators asked for new contract provisions which would permit the packing corporation to continue its compulsory retirement policy. The parties could not resolve this and other differences with the result that a seven-day strike ensued. The new contract which was signed included a special provision authorizing the packing corporation (which was merely one of the members of the employers' association in whose name the contract was signed) to retain its retirement policy.[91] The issue has not been raised again.

In the same year, the Fruit and Vegetable Cannery workers became involved in an almost identical dispute with a number of fruit and vegetable canners[92] who also sought to reinstitute the automatic retirement practice which, as in the case just discussed, had been abandoned in response to the manpower shortage during the World War II period. Again in response to the complaints of several members who were being pensioned off with very small benefits, the unions objected to the companies involved. Union officials questioned in the survey alluded to company hints at discontinuation of the several pension plans in the industry if the retirement practices could not be followed. The final compromise resulted in a contract provision which permits automatic retirement of regular employees at age 65 but which also permits these persons to be employed as seasonal workers.

As in the case of the unions in fish and fruit and vegetable canning industries, the warehouse union deals with a large number of employers only a small proportion of whom offer pension plans. Some of these enforce a fixed retirement age. A grievance involving the retirement of two employees occurred shortly after the war in one of the liquor warehouses. The employees declared that they wished to continue on the job; the union then challenged the company's right to retire the men. Eventually a cash settlement was made, the two employees agreeing to "renounce

[91] A union official questioned later, stated that during the strike the two workers involved in the arbitration proceedings approached the union and announced their intention to resign from work rather than permit themselves to be the cause for prolongation of the strike. Company negotiators questioned later noted that severe pressure was applied to the union when the company threatened to discontinue its pension plan entirely if it could not retain the automatic retirement provision.

[92] Of which the one mentioned in connection with fish canning was the largest.

their seniority rights" (as the union official put it) and the case was closed. The fact that other employment was available for the two men was offered as one of the reasons in explanation of the decision not to press the case. A further reason given was that the union was aware that arbitration decisions have gone both ways and was therefore uncertain about the gains to be had through this course. Automatic retirement provisions continue in effect in the industry.[93]

The machinists union is similar to those just discussed in that it deals with a large number of separate employers only some of whom have instituted pension plans. Union officials report that none of the plans in Bay area incorporate compulsory retirement features though in isolated instances employers have sought to have them instituted. In general the issue has been a minor one for the union, not only as a result of the relative paucity of pension plans but also because until very recently there has been a pronounced shortage of machinists in the area.

Two unions covered by the present survey successfully stipulated for non-automatic retirement provisions in pension plans which are industry wide in coverage.

In the recently instituted pension plan secured for the Sailors Union of the Pacific, the normal retirement age is 65 though reduced pensions are available at age 60 and over. At union request, no automatic retirement provision was included in the plan and the employers association, according to both union and employer spokesmen, was perfectly willing to accept this arrangement. As previously indicated, sailors are subject to rather rigorous physical examinations prior to each voyage so that, although they are protected against adverse discrimination on the basis of age alone, the employers are protected against deterioration of their work force through age protected by voluntary retirement conditions.

In the steel industry, voluntary retirement was instituted only after a long period of disagreement. Prior to World War II,

---

[93] The most recent negotiations between the union and the large employers association in the warehousing industry have resulted in the establishment of a pension program. The proposal put forward by the union included a benefit of $100 per month after 25 years of service at age 65, with retirement to be compulsory at age 65 for those entitled to the full pension.

the United States Steel Company had followed a compulsory retirement policy to which the union had for a long time expressed opposition. The policy was withdrawn in the face of the labor shortage brought on by the war. Reinstitution of the practice, shortly after the war, again met with union objection. The union, which claimed that the retirements violated the seniority provisions of the contract, was carrying specific complaints through the grievance machinery, presumably in preparation for their submission to arbitration, when the question again arose in the pension negotiations of 1949. At length, the company agreed to forsake the policy of automatic retirement. The present arrangement, reaffirmed in the 1954 negotiations, empowers the company to request the retirement of individuals whose work performance suggests that retirement is warranted; in such instances, the union is consulted and a joint determination is made.

In the automobile industry, the major pension plans call for automatic retirement at age 68. This was the pattern established in the Ford settlement in 1949 and incorporated in the Chrysler and General Motors pension agreements which followed shortly thereafter.

In July 1952 an "Administrative Letter" over the signature of Walter Reuther laid down UAW policy on compulsory retirement and reviewed the history of the issue.[94]

Where compulsory retirement provisions appear in our pension plans, it is only because of management insistence. Both the International and UAW Local Unions fought hard and long against compulsory retirement features; and we were finally compelled to concede them in order to establish the first pension programs in our collective bargaining contracts.

The Reuther statement came at a time when, according to some local officers, a considerable amount of resentment against the compulsory retirement provisions was being generated among a large number of older auto workers, and when in the period immediately ahead, the compulsory retirement provisions in some other plans to which the union was signatory were going into effect.[95] The letter continued with the statement that "It is the

---

[94] *UAW-CIO Administrative Letter,* July 1, 1952, p. 1.
[95] During the period, March 1, 1950, until October 30, 1952, some 24,500 workers were retired under UAW pension plans. Of these 7,250 were retired at or over 68

firm purpose of the International Union to assist Local Unions in every way to negotiate the removal of compulsory retirement provisions from UAW-CIO pension agreements at the earliest possible opportunity.[96] And more recent union policy statements have reaffirmed this position.[97]

There is some evidence that the UAW position was not always so firmly established on the principle of compulsory retirement. Local officials in the Bay area declared that union attitudes have undergone some change since the first major pension agreements were negotiated. Two, in fact, referred to a "reversal" in union policy and stated that higher union officials at one point looked with favor upon the prospect of the exit of older workers, because there was general concern among the union's leadership over the prospect of an oncoming depression at the time the first pensions were negotiated.[98]

Whatever earlier doubts about proper policy may have existed, the union's current activities seem definitely oriented toward the elimination of existing compulsory retirement provisions. In his statement to the 1953 UAW Convention, Reuther called attention to the fact that ". . . through voluntary renegotiation. . . . [such provisions] . . . . have already been eliminated from a number of UAW pension agreements which initially included them."[99] And recent statistics dealing with the more than 200 separate plans in which the union participates indicates progress along the path

years of age. *United Automobile Worker,* January 1953. There is no way to determine how many of the 7,250 were involuntarily retired. However, some indication of the possible magnitudes may be inferred from the fact that while there had been 15,700 voluntary retirements on the part of workers between the ages of 65 and 68, over the two and one-half year period, an estimated 17,000 workers between 65 and 68 were still on the job at the end of the period. *Ibid.*

[96] *UAW-CIO Administrative Letter,* July 1, 1952, p. 3.

[97] "The UAW will continue to oppose automatic or compulsory retirement based on age alone and will seek to eliminate such clauses which now exist because of necessary compromises in collective bargaining." *Proceedings,* statement of Walter Reuther to the UAW convention (March 22–27, 1953), p. 20.

[98] According to one source, "The UAW had no objection to the compulsory retirement at 68 contained in the Ford Pension Plan and has proposed contracts to other companies containing automatic retirement clauses." *Industrial Bulletin* (New York State Department of Labor, September, 1950). At least one other observer has commented on what he interpreted as a failure of the union to oppose the compulsory retirement provision in the original Ford plan. See Whittlesey, *op. cit.*

[99] *Proceedings:* statement of Walter Reuther to the UAW convention (March 22–27, 1953), p. 20.

of elimination of the classes. As indicated in Table III, about one-fifth of the plans contained no compulsory retirement provisions at the later date while only one-sixth had no such provisions two and a half years earlier. It should not be overlooked that in virtually all of the plans permitting compulsory retirement the critical age was 68 or over, in comparison to the vast majority of unilateral and negotiated plans in which the automatic retirement age is set at 65.

TABLE III

RETIREMENT PROVISIONS IN UAW PENSION PLANS

| Compulsory Retirement Age | Number of Plans in Effect | |
|---|---|---|
| | January 1, 1951 | July 1, 1953 |
| 65...................... | 3 | 4 |
| 66...................... | 1 | 1 |
| 68...................... | 100 | 143 |
| 69...................... | 2 | 3 |
| 70...................... | 4 | 11 |
| None................... | 22 | 43 |
| Total............. | 132 | 205 |

SOURCE: J. Perham Stanley, "Pension Plans Negotiated by the UAW-CIO" *Monthly Labor Review*, 77 (January, 1954), 13.

## Indifference to or Sponsorship of Compulsory Retirement

There were some notable exceptions to the generally negative attitude toward compulsory retirement just described. With some qualifications to be noted later, unions in three industries, electric and gas utilities, telephone and oil refining, have had relatively long records of indifference to the compulsory retirement provisions prevailing in the pension plans of their respective employers.

The electrical workers local representing the employees of the large gas and electric utility company in the Bay region has expressed little interest in the company's compulsory retirement policy. The major reason, apparently, is that there has been little or no membership objection to the policy. The local's president reported that a mailed questionnaire sent out to his membership, asking for suggestions in connection with bargaining demands, drew a thirty per cent response but that he remembered not a single comment concerning compulsory retirement, though there was considerable sentiment for early retirement.

This appraisal of the membership sentiment seems, at least, to have been the one acted on by the union leadership in the presentation of its pension demands to the company. The local which, only a short while previously, had won bargaining rights after a bitter struggle with another union, submitted a well-publicized 12-point proposal for improvement of the pension plan. There was strong incentive to demonstrate to the rank and file that the new leadership was seeking to advance the interests of the membership. Yet, there was no mention of altering the compulsory retirement policy. One of the proposals, did, however, ask for liberalized early retirement provisions.

The reasons advanced by the local president for the lack of interest in the compulsory retirement policy were as follows:

1. Employment in the industry is generally steady and job security is high. As a result, by the time most employees reach the age of 65 they are to some degree at least financially secure.

2. Pension benefits of the contributory plans are high relative to most industrial pensions so that retiring workers are relatively secure financially for this reason alone.

3. A large part of the membership is in rural areas where gardening, small scale farming, community interests and other activities are available to keep pensioners busy so that retirement does not weigh on them.

In fact, these reasons contributed to pressure for more liberal early retirement provisions. One great virtue of early retirement from the point of view of the workers is that those who can get jobs elsewhere are able to draw their pensions while at the same time they earn a full salary from the new employer which may be as large or larger than the one being earned from the utility company. When employment conditions are very good, and the workers are not particularly troubled by the loss of their job security, the pressure for early retirement is most noticeable.

The situation among telephone workers is in some respects the same as that described for the utility workers and the position of the union has for many years been similar to that of the electrical workers. Ever since 1947 when the first coherent national bargaining program was formulated by the leading union in the industry, the demand for pension reform has centered on three major proposals:

1. improved benefits
2. participation of the union in the administration of the plan
3. more liberal early retirement provisions.

In 1952, opposition of the union to compulsory retirement was voiced officially for the first time. Thus it is not exactly accurate to characterize the union as currently "indifferent" to the principle of automatic retirement. However, it is still true that this feature is a secondary one compared to the other three.

Steadiness of employment and high job security are characteristic of the telephone industry, but unlike the pension plan in the utility company in the Bay area, the telephone pension plan is not a contributory one and the benefits are considerably lower than those of the electrical workers. This is especially true in the case of women whose wages in the telephone industry are much below those of the men and whose pensions as a result are considerably lower.

Early retirement demands arise, in the case of the men, for reasons similar to those discussed in the case of the utility workers. Many have entered at early ages and have accumulated as many as forty years of steady employment with the company by the time they reach their late fifties. Some, having achieved a measure of economic security, are anxious to retire from work completely, while others desire to receive the pension though they intend to work elsewhere.

The situation of the Building Service Workers is rather unique in that a number of its locals are heavily loaded with older workers who have spent many years in other—often skilled— trades but who at the end of their working lives serve as janitors or elevator operators or in similar capacities. A high official of the union expressed the following sentiments (slightly rephrased) concerning compulsory retirement: "Only a small percentage of our people are covered by pension plans. Where compulsory retirement is attached to these plans the affected employee is usually content to be released and to collect his pension. If he wants to continue to work and he is able to do so, he will simply show up at the union and wait to be dispatched to another job. In fact, the chances are that he will 'retire' as soon as he is eligible so that he can receive both the pension and his salary at the new job. We have had no complaints about compulsory retirement from our members. If we should get some we would probably try to do something about it."

Three locals of the oil refinery workers operate in the Bay area. Officials of two of these locals declared that their memberships were offering no complaints against the compulsory retirement policies enforced by the two companies whose workers were represented, and that in the absence of any such protest the leadership saw no reason to object. The reasons offered for the lack of protest were similar to those mentioned in connection with the telephone and utility industries. In the first place, employment was very steady for the long-service people—the rather moderate seasonal fluctuations were absorbed wholly by temporary employees. Thus most of the older workers had had the benefit of regular incomes over a long period of time. In addition to this, the retirement programs of the two companies were extremely well developed so that quite substantial retirement incomes were available to pensioners.

In the third local a somewhat different experience was reported. The pension program of the company represented by this local was a noncontributory plan which for many years was considerably inferior to that of the other two companies. But no compulsory retirement program was enforced, and a substantial number of persons past the age of 65 were continuing in employment. In 1950 a voluntary contributory plan was instituted, but the union, which for several years had been demanding higher benefits at the normal retirement age and a liberal early retirement pension schedule, did not endorse it. Many individual workers participated in the new plan, however. Early in 1954 the company decided to enforce a compulsory retirement policy and discharge 23 over-age employees represented by the local union. These discharges were contested by the union which claimed that they were violations of the seniority provisions in the contract. The company claimed that the matter was not subject to arbitration. At length an arbitrator ruled that the matter was subject to arbitration. Shortly thereafter, the union and the company reached broad agreement on the pension plan itself. The membership of the union voted to accept the company program and as a result endorsed the company's right to enforce retirement after age 65. According to the company's personnel director, the 23 persons involved in the grievance are no longer working for the company.

The same company official disclosed that when layoffs occurred in 1953 in one of the refineries outside of the Bay area a delegation of the local union officers visited him to request that compulsory retirement provisions be invoked at the affected refinery. In this particular industry, therefore, all three attitudes toward compulsory retirement—indifference, opposition and sponsorship—seem to have been held at almost the same time by the various locals.

A compulsory retirement provision was sponsored by the longshore union in the pension plan which it won for waterfront workers in 1952. The circumstances surrounding that program have been discussed. The extreme policy seems to have been the product mainly of two factors which may not recur. First, the longshoremen included an exceptionally large number of aged men. Secondly, the union underestimated the proportion of those men who would retire voluntarily. Moreover, the threat of underemployment was relatively severe. Local officials have indicated that future pension programs in the industry may not incorporate the compulsory retirement feature, because the special need for it will have passed.

## SUMMARY AND CONCLUSIONS

A view widely held and often expressed several years ago was that the mushrooming of collectively bargained pension programs was a special response to the wage stabilization program in effect during the Korean War. Many observers saw the drive for private pension plans as primarily a stop-gap tactic and forecast that pension programs would not find a permanent place in union bargaining demands.[100] Yet, other observers had perceived strong union pressures for pension programs well before the outbreak of the Korean War and the formation of the wage stabilization program. The explanations which they offered and which have been summarized briefly in an earlier section were based on far from ephemeral phenomena. It may be too early to say that this view of the nature of the union demand for pensions has been fully vindicated, but it is certainly true that the pension demand has been persistent and strongly in evidence since the end of the stabilization program. The present investigation was in part an attempt to gain some further understanding of the pressures behind the pension demands. On the whole, the evidence tended to support the view that these demands are deeply rooted.

Early in the pension drive there was a rather general expectation that unions would experience intense internal conflict over the question of the installation and the magnitude—where they exist already—of pension benefit programs. The present study failed to turn up evidence of severe internal differences on the

[100] See Harold W. Davey, *Contemporary Collective Bargaining* (New York: Prentice Hall, 1951), pp. 211–212, for a review of this position.

issue. It is possible that union officials, the main sources of information on this subject, have systematically understated the degree of internal conflict but it is doubtful that they could have completely censored it. There are too many ways in which its presence, if strong, can make itself known—even to the outsider. The evidence seemed to indicate that many workers not eligible for pension benefits for many years were nevertheless favorably inclined to the institution of pension programs. And others were neutral or passive even though the pensions to which they would not be eligible for decades were being purchased with money that might have gone toward current wages. It is likely that a considerable portion of this passivity can be attributed to a willingness to do something for the older workers, especially where such a willingness has been equated to action in conformity with "union principles." Union leaderships characteristically have presented pensions in these terms, and there seem to have been large numbers who have accepted them in this way.

But another and perhaps stronger reason for the favorable attitudes of younger workers toward pensions is that pensions are effective devices to induce older workers to leave the labor market and thus throw open easier or higher paying jobs on the one hand while generally enhancing the job security of those remaining at work, on the other. It is known as a result of mobility studies and other researches into worker attitudes toward their jobs that security of employment has the highest rank in the worker's scale of values and that it will be sought even at the cost of considerable wage sacrifice. The earlier forecasts of heavy internal strife on the pension issue apparently failed to give adequate weight to this consideration.

The study indicated that union officials, the incumbent leadership, have taken an active role in the sponsorship and defense of pension programs. Most local officials who were interviewed in the course of the investigation expressed themselves strongly in favor of the programs. But the evidence was not limited to the interview response. Apart from humanitarian considerations—and in this case, the officials appear to be influenced by them—there are two important reasons for the favorable attitudes toward pension programs which union officials exhibit.

In the first place, pension programs secured by the union through collective bargaining are represented as important achievements, and apparently serve as a solidifying force. Union officials are pleased to advertise the economic achievements of their organizations and the degree of attention which pension systems have merited in the union publications indicates that they are regarded by the membership as valuable additions to their welfare. Further, the increased "institutionalization" of the union by virtue of its participation in the administration of the plans seems to be a consideration of importance.

Secondly, pension programs seem to be valued by union officials as devices to drain older workers out of the labor market. Many officials frankly acknowledged their view of retirement programs as designed, in part, to perform this function, even if they did not generally discuss this function with reference to their organization's and their own security. The presence of unemployment provides the opportunity for the test of this hypothesis, and in a number of the labor markets investigated, union officials have demonstrated a remarkable sensitivity to unemployment and a tendency to turn to pensions as one of the devices to deal with it. Unemployment gives rise to internal political pressures and often to the emergence of factions which spring up along older divisive lines as well as on the newer economic issues. A union's security is endangered by the presence of persistent unemployment in the labor market in which it operates; the union leadership's security is derived in part from the security of the organization as a whole, and even more directly from leadership ability to head off sources of dissatisfaction among the membership. From either point of view, a generous pension benefit program turns out to be a useful defensive device.

The importance of employment (and unemployment) considerations for union pension policy was emphasized by the investigation of union attitudes toward retirement provisions and especially compulsory retirement. In general, union sentiment was opposed to compulsory retirement, but there was considerable variation in the degree of opposition, and further, there were some unions which were quite indifferent to the compulsion aspect.[101]

[101] Opposition tended to be most pronounced where pension benefits were relatively low. The traditional antipathy to compulsory retirement seems to have been

[ 83 ]

Very revealing were the two instances in which unions actively sponsored the institution of a compulsory retirement policy. In each, the policy seems to be traceable primarily to a context of unemployment and the pressures which emerged from it. In addition to this, union interest in liberal early retirement provisions was found in several instances to have been especially stimulated by unemployment or the threat of unemployment. Finally, rules prohibiting pensioners from working in the labor market of the pensioning union (but not in others!) offer additional evidence of the importance of employment considerations in the formation of union pension policy.

The problems raised for the union by cyclical fluctuations and resulting unemployment accentuate the relationships between pension policy and the complex of policies affecting older worker employment opportunity discussed in Part I and summarized on pages 42–46. Unions customarily confer protection on their older members, but this enhanced employment opportunity usually costs something in terms of younger worker convenience, employer good will, or even wage and conditions levels. The "decision" governing the size of this subsidy is, of course, always subject to reconsideration; it is likely to be sharply revised when conditions worsen within the union's labor market. And at the extreme when substantial unemployment threatens, a crisis is at hand. On whom within the union shall the burden of unemployment fall? Who shall subsidize whom, in this most valuable of currencies?

One clear alternative for the union is to permit the seniority and similar systems to effect the necessary adjustment. But another obvious alternative is to attempt to induce the older workers to leave the work force through retirement.

To what degree are present pension programs designed to relieve the pressure of the employment volume adjustment from the seniority and similar internal priority systems currently in effect in many labor markets? There are at least two major speculations which would provide an *a priori* basis for supposing that

based, to a large extent, upon a reluctance to permit oldsters to be stranded without adequate income, and not mainly upon opposition to compulsion, *per se*. As retirement incomes have risen, so has union acceptance of automatic retirement schemes.

pension systems have become increasingly attractive from this point of view. It has been suggested, for one thing, that as the unions become more securely established in their respective labor markets through having gained either employer acceptance or resignation to their presence, the union security function performed by seniority systems, inflexible dispatching procedures, prohibitions against physical examinations, etc., becomes less important and there is less need therefore to insist on the stronger versions of the controls normally applied in these spheres, e.g., strict seniority in layoffs. It is suggested also that unions are operating in an era in which it has become especially important to find new ways to secure the allegiance of the wage earners and particularly the younger ones who enter employment relatively unimpressed with what the "old timers" may choose to regard as the union's achievements, and unburdened with attitudes or recollections which cause them to fear or distrust the employers, the latter having moderated to a great degree many of the practices which inspired anti-employer feeling and union solidarity at an earlier time. The presence of seniority systems which are clear discriminations against the younger worker may turn out to be dangerously divisive in such a context. A pension system which relieves internal pressures through inducing the older workers to exit from the work force may be correspondingly attractive as a solution to the problems set up by the desire to protect the older workers, on the one hand, and the wish to minimize internal and external conflict, on the other.

The findings of the present study were certainly consistent with these speculations though they were too fragmentary and limited to go very far toward establishing their soundness. On the whole, the employment declines in the labor markets studied were relatively mild and the period of observation was relatively short. Despite this, the pension "solution" as a response to unemployment or even anticipations of it was clearly in evidence.

A word concerning the relevance of the present investigation to recent discussions of union wage policy is in order here. A leading question in the debate has been whether or not prospective unemployment deters unions from making "irresponsible" wage demands. Our study tends to confirm the proposition that unions

[ 85 ]

are sensitive to unemployment and that they tailor their bargaining programs so as to cope with it. But as Reder has emphasized,[102] this does not necessarily refute Ross's original contention that ". . . the wage bargain must almost always be made without consideration of its employment effect."[103] What the present study suggests is that if a union wished to enjoy the fruits of "irresponsibility" without necessarily paying the traditional bitter price, unemployment, it might succeed if it devoted large enough fractions of its irresponsibly large, annual bargaining gains to pensions. Retirements might, for a time at least, handily balance the resultant decline in employment.

The question was posed at the outset whether there is a unique union position on the extent to which the community as a whole should underwrite the leisure and well-being of the elderly. If society must choose between a relatively high and a relatively low "economic burden," as defined above, for which alternative is the union vote likely to be cast? The answer seems to be that by and large, unions are making implicit choices for a relatively high economic burden. Our study suggests that the policies which have led them to this position are deeply rooted and will not be easily reversed. On the other hand, as long as it is true that pension systems are a means to an end as well as an end in themselves, the possibility remains that they will be supplanted, to some degree, by other programs which perform the same or similar functions. It is reasonable to expect, for example, that the spread of "guaranteed annual wage" programs will result in some loss of "steam" behind the pension drive, because the immediate effect of these guarantees is to remove the sting from unemployment. If "seniority" is a subsidy to the older union members, the guaranteed annual wage confers greater than proportional benefits upon the younger low-seniority men. The latter may be less inclined to countenance expensive pensions in a situation in which prospective layoffs are not associated with sharp drops in take-home pay. This speculation must be modified, however, by the recognition of the fact that quite apart from the un-

---

[102] M. W. Reder, "The Theory of Union Wage Policy," *The Review of Economics and Statistics*, XXXIV (February, 1952), pp. 42 ff.

[103] Arthur M. Ross, *Trade Union Wage Policy*, (Berkeley: University of California Press, 1948), p. 90.

employment stimulus there are substantial "institutional" as well as powerful welfare reasons for the pension demands.[104]

A general conclusion which emerges from our survey is that union pension and retirement policies are still very much in the process of development. The diverse and changing attitudes toward compulsory retirement offer an impressive case in point. Some unions have plunged enthusiastically into extensive pension programs. Others have been more than hesitant about taking the initial steps. Meanwhile, there has been a growing recognition of the great expense that reasonably adequate pensions entail. But it is not at all clear that leaderships and memberships have made equally sober evaluations of the gains vs. the costs of the plans. Actually, the dust is just beginning to settle from the first great surge into the pension domain. It is still a little too early for definitive answers to the questions addressed by the present study.

---

[104] It is a striking fact that while the "guaranteed annual wage" monopolized headlines in the 1955 automobile industry negotiations, the union gave no evidence of lessening the pressure behind its pension demand. The well-publicized wage guarantee was allocated 5 cents per hour of a "package" said to amount to about 20 cents. At the same time, pension improvements merited 4.5 cents of the same package.